TAX STYLES OF THE RICH AND FAMOUS

7 Ways to Imitate Them and Beat the Tax Man
America's tax "Jedi" tell their secrets

Glenn S. Freed, Ph.D., CPA
and
Charles W. Swenson, Ph.D., CPA,
with
Chris Swenson-Lugo

Writers Club Press
San Jose · New York · Lincoln · Shanghai

Tax Styles of the Rich and Famous
7 Ways to Imitate Them and Beat the Tax Man

ISBN: 0-595-09055-9

Published by Writers Club Press, an imprint of iUniverse.com, Inc.

For information address:
iUniverse.com, Inc.
620 North 48th Street
Suite 201
Lincoln, NE 68504-3467
www.iuniverse.com

URL: http://www.writersclub.com

"How can I get huge tax breaks just like rich people?"

Many people ask themselves this question all the time. The surprising answer is: by imitating them, on a smaller scale. **TAX STYLES OF THE RICH AND FAMOUS** reveals 7 ways the average person can reap such tax benefits.

The authors have spent years studying tax breaks for the wealthy. In fact, they teach it! Freed and Swenson are practicing CPAs who teach graduate tax courses at the third-ranked (nationally!!) tax college program. Their students become tax CPAs and lawyers who then use these ideas, and modify them, to create tax breaks for their wealthy clients. Often, the authors' former students contact their master professors for advice on structuring these breaks.

You will learn, for example, that your favorite hobby can be turned into a tax shelter; that you can create tax breaks from stock trading just like the Wall Street big shots; how to use real estate tax breaks to create wealth; how to exploit the tax law to save for retirement; plus many other tax tricks the authors want to share with you.

Table of Contents

Chapter 1

Introduction

Knowledge itself is power.
—Francis Bacon
What you don't know won't hurt you.
—Some loser who didn't read this book

About a year ago, my brother, the "tax Jedi" (he makes us call him that on holidays…just kidding!), asked me to co-author a book on tax shelters that would be understandable for the general population (that's me and you) but contain basically the same information that's used by people who live in mansions, fly in private jets and never have to think about their own tax returns. He figured if a social worker (call me the "poverty guru") could understand the concepts well enough to write about them, than anyone could take this information and apply it in real life, saving significantly on the amount of taxes they pay each year. I did understand it. You will, too.

First, let's get you riled up with some facts you might not know, but which have definitely been hurting you:

In 1996, Americans paid $11 trillion in taxes of all kinds. (In round numbers. A trillion, by the way, is a one followed by 12 zeros!)

That comes out to $12,118 per household, or 27.2% of a household's income.[1] And, it also means that on average, you worked about **1/3 of the year just to pay taxes**. Doesn't it make you feel good to know that you worked all those days last year just to pay Uncle Sam? And will probably work a couple of more extra days this year!)

You might be interested to know that it wasn't always like this. Did you know that our country has tried imposing income taxes without success for a long time? Taxation without representation was so imbedded in the American psyche since the beginning of this country…that there were 3 different attempts by Congress to impose taxes in the first 100 years of our nation's existence, all of which were shot down in Congress.

In fact, the Supreme Court declared the income tax unconstitutional in 1895.

America finally got over this aversion to taking our money in the year 1913. That's when the states ratified the Sixteenth Amendment to the Constitution…which allowed the government to levy a tax on our incomes.

The Boston Tea Party had occurred 130 years earlier, and its message seems to have gotten lost over time.

Finally, an interesting statistic is that the IRS says that it should take approximately six hours to complete a 1040 with all the schedules. If any of you have fairly complicated returns, we find this figure to be somewhat on the joke side. We know how much time our colleagues spend doing

---

1   From The Statistical Abstract of the U.S., 1998, U.S. Dept. of Commerce.

returns, and we used to do it all day for a living. The IRS is being a little too optimistic with their estimates.

What's the bottom line? A survey by the Roper Center said that 60% of Americans expect to pay more in taxes this year and only 6% think that they will pay less. Also, Americans who think that their taxes are too high represent 55% of Americans.

We could tell you that without even taking a formal survey. Taxes are going up, and are going to continue to go up…unless you do everything you can to fight them legally! That's your money, for your family, and your retirement, being sent to Washington on a one way trip.

To get you even more upset, some wealthy people pay an effective tax rate which is even *lower* than your own!

OK, are you riled up? Are you ready to revolt without lifting a single crate of tea, without inflicting the wrath of the Boston harbor police? In fact, the 7 tax secrets of the wealthy that are outlined in the following chapters are completely legal and can be used by any taxpayer. First, we'll introduce you to some rich and famous people (sorry, no real names, but have fun guessing) and show you what they do to save big bucks on taxes. Then, we'll give you examples of people just like you who used the same legitimate tax deductions to hold on to some of their own hard-earned money. We'll start with something everyone knows about—hobbies—and work our way up to trusts and stock trading. Use just one of these ideas or all of them, and you'll be on the road to taking control of your money.

Chapter 2

Having a Hobby for Fun and No Profit

Do you have an "I brake for yard sales" sticker on your bumper? Is there a new litter of puppies in your garage three times a year? Is your idea of a weekend hotspot the local crafts supply store? Yes? OK, you're definitely not living the "lifestyle" of the rich and famous, but you can imitate their tax styles in ways you probably never considered, just by having a hobby. First, go put some fresh newspaper down in the garage, then read how the Learjet crowd deducts their "hobbies," and finally, see how you can turn your favorite pastimes into real tax deductions.

PAUL

Years ago, Paul started a small magazine out of his garage. Now, he owns a magazine-publishing empire worth hundreds of millions. Paul really likes cars and used some of his millions to indulge his hobby. After his first million, he bought a vintage 1958 Corvette. Soon, his car collection grew to 10, and now numbers near a hundred. He started renting his cars out to movie producers and advertisers when they needed a vintage exotic car. On advice of his tax counsel, he reported the rental fees on his tax returns as income. But, he also deducted every **ordinary, necessary, and reasonable amount** related to his car collection "business." Here are some of the costs he deducted:

- Trips to exotic car shows, where he bought and occasionally sold cars. The trips included all airfare, hotel bills, food, and a portion of his "entertainment" of potential buyers and sellers. Of course, many of the show locations were in interesting places, such as Florida (in winter), and Hawaii.
- All expenses directly related to the cars: insurance, maintenance, licenses, etc.
- **Depreciation (*remember this word*)**. This is the amount by which the cars presumably went down in value over time. This is a "paper" write-off, and requires no cash outlays.
- All costs related to his "museum" which housed the cars. The museum, until very recently, was located next to his mansion. Costs included utilities, insurance, and depreciation.

When the costs were subtracted from the revenues, they usually generated a net loss. The tax savings, which reduced his tax bill from his profits from investments and his magazine empire, often were in seven figures. And the best part: the losses weren't out-of-pocket losses, since they were generated, in large part, by the "paper" losses from depreciation.

JERRY

Remember the 1960's TV show, "Green Acres"? Eddie Albert was a New York City lawyer, who lived on an upstate New York farm with his wife, Eva Gabor.

Well, his counterparts exist. Meet Jerry—a partner in the New York office of one of the world's largest CPA firms. Jerry makes well into seven figures each year. During the week he stays in a NYC apartment , but his real home is set in the middle of his "farm" in the heart of the beautiful Connecticut countryside. You wouldn't know that it's a farm—there are unplowed fields, idle equipment, a barn badly in need of repainting, no pig named Arnold, etc. There are apple orchards and vineyards which are harvested each year by a company that comes through and does the work. The company pays Jerry a net amount, which is the market value of the harvest, less the costs of harvesting. Of course, he reports this net amount as income each year on his tax return. But, the income is almost always much smaller than the expenses related to the farm. The expenses include:

- Depreciation on the barn, the equipment, the fences and outside walls, etc.
- Costs of water and fertilizer for the "crops."
- Costs of putting in drainage systems, clearing out unwanted shrubs and trees, and paving an area adjacent to the barn, for equipment (Jerry's family actually plays roller hockey and volleyball in this area when not used by the "equipment").

In an average year, the tax savings from this farm is about $100,000. Of course, much of the "loss" is really just on paper, from depreciation. Wouldn't it be nice to tax deduct the cost of maintaining your yard, too? It's expensive replacing those pink flamingoes, isn't it?

JILL

Jill is an actress who, at age 50, has accumulated enough money from movies and TV appearances to live off of her investments. Just outside her rural Los Angeles-area home is a large thoroughbred horse facility, where Jill has horses. Lots of them. She has always loved horses, and one of her "businesses" is to breed and race thoroughbreds. Sometimes her horses place in a race, which pays well. But, usually her investment loses money each year, especially when she sells a horse which is past its prime (sort of like Jill, in the current Hollywood climate!). Here are some of the expenses Jill reports on her taxes:

- Travels to/from races around the country, including meals, hotel, and airfare
- All costs of maintaining the horses—food, trainers, tack, etc.
- Depreciation on the horses—that's right, you can write them off (and no, if any producers are reading this, you cannot deduct depreciation on your actresses...and for God's sake, give Jill a job; she's got more talent in her little finger than all those teeny-bopper bimbos you've been hiring...whoops, we've digressed).

All tolled, Jill saves about $200,000 each year in taxes from this "business," which reduces her tax bill from her other investments, and royalty checks. You go, Jill! We loved you in...sorry, can't say, but you know which movie we mean! Wouldn't it be nice if we could travel around and deduct our traveling costs?

BILL

Bill had burned out. We don't mean sort of, we mean like a used up candle. He was fried.

And, the most amazing this is that Bill was (is) a very successful dentist. Very successful. He is 43 years old, and had a thriving practice grossing over a million dollars a year. He had all the trappings of success. The Mercedes. The vacation home. The kids in fancy schools. The "deluxe" macaroni and cheese instead of the "3 for $1" brand, even between paydays!

But, Bill was miserable. He actually hated being a dentist. In fact, he enrolled in dental school because his dad was a dentist, and both parents pushed him to follow in his dad's footsteps.

"You'll love it," they kept telling him. Well, Bill didn't love it at all. He understood that being a dentist was a noble and worthwhile profession. But it just wasn't for him. Not only that, he had a very tough time running the business side of things (collecting money from insurance companies, hiring staff, etc.).

Bill's wife Carol, by the way, didn't like that *he* didn't like being a dentist. As a matter of fact, they had some interesting conversations every time he mentioned he wanted out of the practice. (Sometimes even loud ones. Sometimes Bill even had to make his own macaroni and cheese!)

Anyway, last year, Bill decided to investigate whether he could get out, what would happen to him if he did, and what options he had available to him. He hired us to work with him, and get him the answers he so desperately wanted to find.

The first thing that was done was a psychological interview to determine how Bill—and his wife—really felt about all kinds of issues and concerns. (Bill got Carol to agree to explore their options before making any moves.)

We put together a series of choices for Bill and Carol to take a hard look at things like the tax consequences of selling the practice (how to reduce them significantly); how much money they needed to set aside for their two teenagers' upcoming college expenses, and whether or not they could afford to keep the vacation home, nice cars, and so forth.

Most of all, we planned out the feasibility of Bill starting a computer consulting business, by himself, out of his home. (He had always loved computers, and was a self taught expert. In fact, he used to talk about computers to most of his patients!) They examined the costs, expenses, projected income, insurance, tax aspects, etc.

The good news is that Bill and Carol both agreed that there was a better than good chance they would be able to get out of the dental business, and into the home based consulting business, *while still maintaining their previous (including macaroni) lifestyle!*

While everyone acknowledges that there are no guarantees in life, this plan made perfect sense. It allowed for their personalities, and for their financial needs. And, even though nothing can be assured, they both felt like the numbers made realistic sense.

Carol remarked that she felt like a weight was lifted off her shoulders. The plan permitted her to stop feeling like she was pressuring Bill, whom she really loved, into continuing a job that made him hate getting up in the morning. Which made her hate getting up as well. The plan showed her how there was a very real chance they would not suffer any unpleasant giant steps backward during the transition.

Anyway, after a month of thinking it over, they decided to give it a go. Bill sold the practice to the woman who came in as his assistant a couple of years ago, and worked a deal for her to buy the entire business over a period of a few years.

Bill paid off the remaining debts with some of this money, and used the balance to start the computer business (which was a joke compared to the giant capital he needed to start his dental practice). Bill isn't making huge profits yet, but he enjoys his new profession. Right now, he's running it out of the detached garage next to his house. The expenses he deducts on his tax return are the usual: utilities, insurance, repairs, depreciation, etc. on the garage. Plus phone, advertising, costs of materials, etc. He formed a separate company (an S corporation) to hold the business, which allows him to do two important things. First, since it's a corporation, if it goes bankrupt or gets sued, his personal assets are safe—only the assets owned by the company can be lost. Second, the company can tax deduct the wages of employees—in this case, wages paid to his wife and daughter! That's right, he can pay his daughter an allowance, and tax deduct it.

Now several months later, they are doing just great. Not just financially either. They are doing well emotionally, and have found secrets to a happy life together (hint…it's not macaroni and cheese)!

ON STARTING A BUSINESS

So what's the secret formula that these rich people possess? The answer is: they're just legitimately using the tax law as it is written! That's right—if you run a business, even if you enjoy doing it, if you're at least trying to make a profit from it, you can deduct the tax losses and save taxes. The key is that you have to really be trying to make a profit. Now, the IRS won't put you on a witness stand to ask you, under oath, whether you really, really meant to make a profit. Instead, they look for these signs that you were really trying to make a profit:

- Whether the activity is conducted in a business-like manner
- The expertise of the person(s) running the business, or their advisors
- The time and effort expended
- The expectation that the business assets will appreciate in value
- The person's previous success in conducting similar activities
- The history of income or losses from the activity
- The relationship of profits earned to losses incurred
- The financial status of the person. For example, if the person does not have substantial amounts of other income, this may indicate that the activity is engaged in for profit.
- Elements of personal pleasure or recreation in the activity.

Of course, for the IRS to challenge you, you have to be audited first. Now, the chances of an audit, on average, are less than 1%! If the tax man does successfully assert that your business was only a hobby, then you can only deduct your expenses to the extent you have income. Your net tax shelter won't work in that case. So, again, the key is to look as if you're trying to make money. In some activities, such as horse racing, only the really big shots make money, so if that's the kind of business you run, you may be off the hook. The IRS also has what's called a "presumptive rule", which says that if you make a profit in any 2 out of 5 year period (2 out of 7 years for horses), the burden of proof is shifted to the IRS to show that you don't have a legitimate business.

So, let's read on about how the average person can imitate the rich people's "businesses"…and it's important to realize here that we can't deduct our hobbies unless they can generate a profit, so lounging on the couch and surfing the cable channels won't qualify, even if you find a quarter under the cushion!

BOB

Bob really loves Labrador retrievers. Can't get enough of 'em. Although he works full time as an electrician, he devotes his weekends to his dogs. At last count, he had twenty. He breeds and sells them, sometimes entering them into dog shows. In an average year, he sells ten at about $400 each. His costs are advertising in newspapers, food, vet care, travel costs to/from dog shows. Also, his garage is converted to a kennel. So, he deducts depreciation, plus part of his house's utilities and insurance related to the garage. Some years he makes a profit, other years he doesn't. Truth is, he would raise Labs anyway. But the tax deductions, which reduce the tax bite on his electricians' wages, sweeten the deal.

SUE

You probably know someone just like Sue. Every Saturday and Sunday, her front lawn and opened garage are filled with ceramics—pots, lamps, vases, etc. As a stay at home mom, she uses her spare time to make ceramics. On weekends, she sells them. For the first four years, her expenses exceeded her income, and the net loss was a tax shelter, reducing the tax bite on her husband's salary. Her deductions include materials, supplies, advertising, business license, utilities/maintenance/insurance attributable to the garage, as well as our old friend depreciation (on the garage).

DOUG

Doug really enjoys yard sales, swap meets, and flea markets. Before going to work each day, he scours the morning newspapers for weekend yard sales and estate sales. He's the guy who's parked at your curb when you open the garage door on Saturday and Sunday mornings. By 10 a.m., he is reselling his purchases at the local swap meet. Since his wife hates clutter, he tries to sell everything by the end of the day. Some weeks he makes a profit, but the truth is he has fun talking with people, wheeling and dealing, and hoping to come across an undervalued "treasure." Since he uses his old truck exclusively for hauling his purchases, he deducts the oil, gas, maintenance, and depreciation attributable to the truck. His other tax deductions include the costs of his yard sale purchases, and the fee he pays to set up a table at the swap meet.

To Lease Or Not To Lease?...

We get asked all the time about car leasing. Should we buy, or lease, and if so, what's the best deal? Etc. Etc. Even if the car is not used in your hobby (oops, business), it can still make sense to lease.

Well, right now, we suggest you take a hard look at leasing, instead of buying. (With the qualification that each individual case merits individual review. These tips are, of course, general, and not meant to apply to anyone in particular. Please contact your financial advisor prior to making a decision about a new car! Then, compare your options and help you decide the best way to go!)

Maybe, you just can't get used to the idea of "buying" a car, making all those payments, and having nothing left to show for it when all is said and done! But let's be realistic here for a moment. What are you getting in return for the money you pay down, and monthly, for a car? With the way prices drop like a hot rock on new cars, it's not uncommon to own a half paid-for car that is worth less than what you owe on it! (Car dealers call this being "upside down" on your vehicle. It happens every day.)

Here's a few reasons to lease:

1. Low, or no money tied up in down payments. (you can invest this money instead of sinking it into a car that is 100% guaranteed to go down in value!)

2. You can get 2-3 year leases with very low finance rates calculated in. (Ask your dealer about promotional leasing deals. They have them all the time. One of our clients just got a 3.9% rate on a 2½ year lease.)

3. A "closed end" lease allows you the option of handing the keys back in at the termination of the lease, or buying the car at a stated "residual" value (this is better than open end leases that require you to buy the car at the end).

4. You can get a new car every few years, never tie up any capital that could be invested elsewhere, and never risk losing a big pile of money on a quickly depreciating car.

5. The interest on car loans isn't deductible on the individual tax forms (unless you own, or use the car for business). So there is no advantage to borrowing money with no tax assistance.

6. With all the cars that have been leased in the last few years, there is going to be a glut of leased cars back in the marketplace, driving used car prices down even further. Buying a car *is not* an investment. It is an expense with a bleak outlook for future improvement.

Make sure you shop and compare. Leases and rates are just as negotiable as the price of the car for purchase (another one of our clients got a dealer down $180 a month from the original asking payment).

If you use the car in your business, even better. The lease payments can be tax deductible!

FINALLY, AFFORDABLE MEDICAL

Most of us can't tax deduct our medical expenses. This is because the total of our payments to doctors, dentists, medical insurance companies, etc must be more than 7.5% of our "adjusted gross income". For the majority of people, there is no deduction unless they have a disastrous health year, or very low income. If you have your own business, however, *every cent the company pays for your medical expenses is deductible by your company.*

SUPERSIZE MY TAX DEDUCTIONS, PLEASE!

When you "go big" on tax deductions, expect some IRS attention. Such was the 1997 US Tax Court case of Stanley M. Kurtzet and Ann Kurtzet

v. Commissioner. At age 53, Stanley sold the stock in his successful business for $20 million in cash. He used the proceeds to buy three projects: a timber farm in Oregon, realty in Tahiti, and a Lear jet. While the Tax Court saw the timber farm as a legitimate business (allowing $3 million in tax losses), the other two issues seemed to cross the line. The oceanfront property in Tahiti, which the Kurtzets traveled to twice a year to visit, resulted in tax deductions of $1.8 million—which the tax court disallowed as a "hobby". Also, the Lear jet (which gave them $1.7 million in tax deductions over 3 years) was disallowed as a deduction, since it was used largely to go to Tahiti and to visit the Kurtzets' condominiums and vacant lots in the ski resorts of Park City, Utah.

JIMMY

Jimmy's comic book and baseball card collection was world famous (at least among his friends and relatives). In his comics collections, he had original Spiderman and Superman issues, and his baseball cards featured rookie season cards for such greats as Willie Mays and Hank Aaron. Finally, everyone persuaded him to start selling them. He converted an existing bedroom in his house to run his new business. On our advice, he deducted all costs related to this room—utilities, phone, part of the house insurance, and of course depreciation—against any income he had from selling his collection. He also deducted al of his costs of going to comic book and baseball card conventions, where he sold (and sometimes bought). His first year, he sold $30,000 worth of his collection, but he didn't have to pay a dime to Uncle Sam, since his expenses (including the original purchase price of his collection) zeroed out his income!

THE "BUSINESS" TOUR

Within limits, deducting part of a leisure trip can be tax deductible, so long as the trip is primarily for business purposes. For example, you can't go to Hawaii and spend 3 days at the beach and one day doing business. On the other hand, if there were three days of business and one of fun, it is much easier. In this case, airfare to and from your destination are deductible. Meals and lodging are 50% deductible, so long as they are directly business related. If you tack your leisure time onto the end of the trip, the hotel is not deductible for the leisure days, unless air fares are lower by staying over on a Saturday night (i.e., there's a real business reason for staying later). If the vacation day or days are sandwiched between business days, you'll have a much easier time deducting hotel, car rental, etc for the vacation days.

If you would like to see how to deduct a hobby on your tax return, there's an example in the Appendix and the end of the book.

Don't stop deducting now. The next chapter instructs you how to get even more tax savings through doing something that gives you the warm-fuzzies.

Chapter 3

Give to Charity, Not Uncle Sam

"Give 'till it hurts" was the plea of many charities in the last 20 years. "Give it to Uncle Sam until it really hurts" is our addition.

Donations are the lifeblood of charitable organizations. They also occupy one of the few soft spots left in Uncle Sam's heart. Such organizations are usually tax-exempt, and donations to them are tax deductible.

Many wealthy people have found ways to fully take advantage of the rules, as the following stories illustrate.

ALISTAIR AND REBECCA

As true "bluebloods", this wealthy couple had a taste for the finer things in life. They especially liked art, and their collections of paintings by the grand masters were estimated to be worth in excess of $100 million. Upon advice of their tax attorney, they founded a museum in the downtown area, from a warehouse they refurbished. Open to the public, the museum was a form of charitable organization known as a private foundation. Alistair and Rebecca received tax deductions for any art which they "donated" to their charity. By donating piecemeal, they saved about $4 million per year in taxes, for 10 years.

We went to the (by invitation only) black tie opening ceremony of their museum, and it was incredible. Hollywood celebs, LA area politicians, photographers. We actually sneaked into the background when photos were taken , just for fun.

"Hey, ya'all, come over here!" called Rebecca. Raised in Charlestown, South Carolina, she retained much of her Southern charm.

"Look at this Matisse. Isn't it incredible!" She exclaimed. It was beautiful. But something was vaguely familiar…Yes! We used to have it…in a jigsaw puzzle as kids!

"Awesome." We said, now that we recognized it.

Alistair and Rebecca are not unusual stories. In fact, many art museums around the country are private foundations, formed and controlled by wealthy individuals. Of course, the art is still appreciated by its original owners, who have private showings, and who have appointed the foundations' board of directors.

Just this last year, much of the luster for private foundations has been lost because of tax law changes limiting the tax deductions. So, instead, the wealthy have turned to something called a "supporting organization", or "SO" for short.

Many celebrities give generously to charities. For example, Oprah Winfrey has donated millions of dollars to higher education institutions such as Morehouse College, Spelman College, and Tennessee State University.

CARL, GERRY, AND DAVID[3]

Ex-corporate raider Carl Icahn turned over $100 million in cash and stock to his SO, and received a tax deduction, while still retaining man-

3   Source: "Gimme Shelter: The SO Trend." Wall Street Journal 5/29/98, p.A1, by Monica Langley.

agement of his stock as if it were his own. Well-known defense lawyer Gerry Spense donated his 220 acre ranch in Wyoming to his SO, while still being able to host meetings with other lawyers there. Real estate investor David Cammack donated his valuable Tucker car collection to his SO, while still deciding when and how they are displayed, keeping them in his garage.

A variation on the private foundation and the SO are charitable lead and remainder trusts. In the former, the individual donates something of value (often, art work) for a fixed time, after which the individual (or his family) gets it back. In a charitable remainder trust, the asset goes to the charity after a fixed period of time. In either case, the individual gets a deduction for part of the value of the asset, while still retaining control and enjoyment.

ROBIN

As the CEO of a successful insurance company, Robin's seven figure compensation put her in the highest tax brackets. Using her connections in the industry, she found out about charitable split-dollar insurance. Under the plan, she made a "gift" to a charity and then took a tax deduction for the amount donated to the charity. The charity then "voluntarily" used the gift to pay the premiums on the life insurance policy for the benefit of Robin's children. When Robin dies, her children and the charity share the death benefit. Robin paid a portion of the premium herself in order to demonstrate that the charity was not paying all the cost of the policy. As with typical policies, the charity would get one-third of the proceeds—hence the name "split dollar". In effect, Robin was getting a tax deductible life insurance policy, something which cannot be done under normal tax rules.

Before rushing out and investing in one of these policies, you should know that Congress just (in December 1999) disallowed the tax benefits of these policies. So, ask your insurance agent if his or her company has developed some other new tax-favored policy!

STAN

Stan is a well-known actor who is active in conservation causes. He spends as little time as possible in his Beverly Hills home, and as much time as possible at his Montana ranch. In an agreement with the county, Stan agreed not to develop 50 acres of his 200 acre ranch, and to keep this area wild. Stan is able to take a tax deduction for ¼ of the value of the land on his ranch, as a "conservation easement." He can still enjoy this land, even if he cannot develop it.

TED

Ted Turner, vice chairman of Time Warner, last year announced that he would give away $100 million annually for ten years to a foundation that would distribute the funds to UN programs. This equates to approximately on-third of his net worth. Mr. Turner's generous gift has given him some ammunition to spur on other wealthy individuals to step up to the plate. He will nonetheless enjoy some benefits of his own from the gift.

Mr. Turner did accomplish some goals through this move. He will avoid any capital gains taxes (by not selling his stock in Time Warner), he will minimize his taxes over the years, and he will still be able to provide for his heirs. Mr. Turner's team of lawyers and accountants will help to maximize the benefits of these goals. Their objective will be to structure the donation to see that the UN charities receive this money and that Mr. Turner receives the maximize his tax benefits.

Mr. Turner wisely decided to make donation of his Time Warner stock instead of cash. When a donation is made in appreciated property, in this case the Time Warner stock, the benefits are maximized because Mr. Turner avoids capital gains taxes while at the same time creating, for himself, a tax deduction against that year's income.

Mr. Turner considered borrowing against the stock to make the donation. This would accomplish the publicly-stated goal of maintaining more than a 10% stake in Time Warner. At the time of his announcement he held approximately 12% of the Time Warner stock. As well, he would still be able to benefit from any increase in the value of the stock. However, he would not be able to deduct the interest on the loan, since the proceeds are considered used for personal purposes.

Mr. Turner's tax benefits are maximized through the donation of appreciated stock. Mr. Turner received his stock at a price of $41.38. Therefore, at the time of the donation, Mr. Turner will be entitled to deduction between this amount and the fair market value of the stock. An additional benefit is that he will avoid the 20% capital gains tax he would have incurred if he were to sell the stock and donate the proceeds.

The entire amount of the gift, the appreciated value of the stock, would qualify as a charitable donation but the amount Mr. Turner can claim in any one year is limited to 20% of his adjusted gross income for that year. As an example, if his AGI is $10 million he could claim a $2 million charitable deduction. If the donation is made through a private foundation, the percent increases to 30%.

Rather than donate directly to the UN, which is not a charitable organization, Mr. Turner can create a private foundation to receive and contribute the gift. If he had decided to give directly to the UN, he would be subject to a gift tax. By directing his donation through the private foundation, Mr. Turner also creates some added benefits. He will be able to maintain some control over the stock and the distribution of the stock. Mr. Turner will be able to have some assurance that his generous gift will be used for the purposes he intended. Mr. Turner's heirs and descendants will also be able to receive salaries as employees of the foundation. This was more than likely an unintended benefit but one that might prove useful in the future. Through the visibility of the foundation, Mr. Turner will also be able to bask in the glow of his gift for many years.

Like these rich peoples' style? Then read on....

BILLY

Everyone has had a neighbor like Billy at on time or another. Constantly under "repair," his three old clunker cars seemed to spend more time in his driveway than on the road. No he didn't make a "museum" out of his front yard ("Pull over, Thelma, I want to get the kids' picture in front of the famous Cars Billy Has Owned Museum! Look—there's the Firebird he almost lost his virginity in!"). He called a local charity, who towed two of them away. Although he would have had a difficult time selling them, he was able to get a tax deduction for their "blue book" values. And what the charity didn't know about the backseat of that Firebird wouldn't hurt them...

JILL

Jill had more clothes and shoes than she could possibly need. Finally, she bit the bullet, and called her local charity. Her tax deduction was for the "fair market value" of the items. Since there is no readily discernable fair market value for such items, she simply deducted the highest value she thought she could. Truth is, the IRS would be unlikely to audit her, and if they did, they would have a hard time disproving her estimates.

MIKE

Mike was a regular giver at his church. This year, he wanted to give the church some stock he held. He had bought the stock five years ago for $10,000, but it kept going down in value, and was now worth only $7,000. If he donated the stock, he could get a tax deduction for the stock's fair market value, or $7,000. Instead, we advised him to first sell the stock, then give the cash to the church. The result: a tax deductible loss of $3000 on the stock, *plus* a charitable contributions deduction of $7000 (Not to mention brownie points with the "Big Guy" upstairs!).

Mike's story is not unusual. Often, the best decision to make, when you have income producing property which has gone down in value but you want to donate it to charity, is to sell the property first to generate a tax deductible loss, then donate the cash to charity.

JIM AND LISA

This couple is actively involved in many organizations—church, PTA, Boy and Girl Scouts—you name it. On our advice, they kept good records of any cash donations they made to these organizations, which added up to about $600. They were also pleasantly surprised to find out that when they paid for tickets to charity banquets, festivals, and fairs, that that the excess of what they paid over the value of the meal (or entertainment) was tax deductible. Also, when they donated any of their personal items to help with special events, these were deductible as well. For example, all the costs of refreshments they served to Cub Scouts (Lisa was a den mother) were deductible. When Dave made a stage for a PTA benefit, all the costs of wood, nails, and paint were deductible. By keeping good records, they came up with an extra $1000 in tax deductions!

If you'd like to see how to deduct contributions, there's an example in the Appendix.

OK, now that you've got two tax-savers under your belt, you're greedy for third, aren't you? So, what're you waiting for...turn the page.

Chapter 4

Guilt-free, Low Tax Real Estate

"Location, location, location" is the chant of successful real estate investors. OK, how 'bout; "Location, location, location...and deduction!". Obsessive? Not us...We'd reverse the order of these four if we were so sick.

Property owners take up that other teeny-tiny soft spot in Uncle Sam's heart, next to the charities. As a result, there are a number of tax benefits which can be used by the wealthy and non-wealthy alike.

ADAM

Like many people whose parents had recently immigrated to the US, Adam was hard-working and willing to make huge sacrifices to accumulate wealth. At age 18, he bought a small flower shop. He saved every penny, and bought a small beach house which he rented out. He wanted to cash out his profits, then reinvest in a larger property.

"Whoa, cowboy, that's a 1031" we warned.

"I've never been convicted yet" he replied.

We really didn't need to know that. Anyway, we informed him that instead of a penal code section, 1031 was a break in the tax code. When the house went up in value, he traded it for a duplex (of course, he had to throw in some extra cash). Because the trade qualified as a so-called "1031 exchange", there were no taxes on the exchange. Adam continued to do this tax free trade-up strategy, until after 20 years, he owned several apartment buildings and two shopping centers, worth about $10 million in total. By trading, instead of selling, then paying taxes on the profit, and using the remaining cash to buy a more valuable property, he was able to reinvest all of his appreciation, and accumulate more wealth.

LAURA

Laura is a successful commercial real estate sales person, earning over $1 million per year. Wanting to become really wealthy, she wanted to purchases a $100 million shopping complex. No bank would loan her that much money.

"How am I gonna catch Donald Trump without a loan?" she joked.

We had to wait to reply because her *second* cell phone was ringing away (she was on the line with us on the other one) while racing her Mercedes convertible somewhere on Pacific Coast Highway. The tone in her voice was the familiar *I want my deal and I want it now rich people thing.*

"REIT!", we blurted out, high-fiving each other with our save. We had her form a real estate investment trust, or REIT. Using her real estate contacts, she found 100 investors (the minimum required for a REIT), who together came up with the $100 million. Under the tax law, a REIT pays no taxes. The investor pays taxes on any dividends which the REIT pays them. Usually, the REIT ties to minimize such distributions; when the investors want to cash out, they simply sell their REIT shares. Although the investors were in the 39% tax bracket, their gains on the sales of their

REIT shares qualified for long-term capital gain treatment—at a maximum tax rate of 20%!

THE REIT WAY, BABY!

Many of our largest hotel-owning companies operate through REITs, saving millions in taxes annually. Many REITs are traded on the NASDAQ, just like shares of stock. The most recent data indicates that the value of such REITS was estimated to over $10 Billion.

SAUL

Like many wealthy movie moguls, Saul held part of his investments in real estate. One of his properties was 10 acres of land. When purchased ten years ago, it was easily 5 miles from the nearest house. Now, it was right in the middle of a number of housing tracts. Saul felt it was time to sell, and he had two choices: sell the land outright for $50 million profit, or build tract homes, and sell them for $75 million profit. The problem with the second option was that the IRS would classify him as a "dealer" in property, and as such he would be subject to the top US tax rate of 39%. When we broke the news, Saul squealed like a porcupine had just given him a prostate exam. Tax first aid time. So, we hatched the following. If he simply sold the land, he would be subject to the long-term capital gain tax rate of 20%. Then, we advised him of a well-known trick: form a limited liability company, or "LLC" (kind of a cross between a partnership and a corporation; could also be a cool name for a rap singer, yo!) with a real estate development company, then sell the land to the company. The gain would be subject to only the 20% tax rate. Next, develop the land into tract homes, and sell them. Only the extra profit would then be subject to the higher 39% rate. Yeah, baby, yeah!

LOU

Lou loved Las Vegas more than Wayne Newton. So much so, that he wanted use part of his fortune (as the major shareholder in a high-tech company) to build a casino-hotel. His vision was a 500 room hotel with a theme (we can't tell you which one, but here's a hint: it has a theme). To get higher tax deductions, just about every internal and external fixture was not permanently attached to the building structure Internal walls could slide; lights were easily unscrewed; signs were bolted (not cemented); and casino equipment was simply screwed into (locked, of course) casino floors and walls. So, all these fixtures could be depreciated over 5,7, or 10 years, instead of 39 years if they had been structurally attached to the building. The result: faster write-offs saved Lou $5 million in taxes his first year alone. Viva depreciation! Now, Lou "comps" our hotel rooms when we visit Lost Wages. Of course, we return it at the blackjack tables. Hey, we never claimed to be *that* smart.

CARLO

Carlo is a well-known entertainer. One of mansions is in the swank LA neighborhood of Bel Air. You'd never realize it's a $15 million dollar tax shelter. That's right—it's owned by Carlo's corporation, which uses it to conduct business—entertain (there is a lovely pool and tennis courts), arrange contracts, etc. The corporation deducts all costs related to the mansion including—you guessed it—depreciation write-offs. Incidentally, Carlo's corporation also owns a Ferrari, which it writes off as well.

DE ISLANDS, MON

Some off-shore island nations (the Bahamas, Netherlands Antilles, etc) have tax treaties with other countries, which keep their residents (including their corporations) from paying taxes on real estate gains in other countries. US companies set up corporations on these islands which (sometimes operating through a complex chain of other companies, such as a Mexico subsidiary) and can avoid paying any taxes on their gains on sales of real estate in the US.

So, excited by what the big boys (and girls) do, and want to get in on the action?

Then read on......

JIM AND EILEEN

Jim had just started a new job in a new city. Flush with cash from the sale of their old home, Jim and Eileen were set on buying a new home for cash. At age 52, Jim didn't want to be saddled with debt so close to retirement. But, here was our advice to them; "The less you need a mortgage, the more you should have one." This is because home mortgage interest is tax deductible[4]; in other words, the higher your tax bracket, the "cheaper" the mortgage becomes. One way to see this is an analysis based on the two highest tax brackets, calculating the rate of return required in the stock market to surpass the mortgage investment. For a person in the 28% bracket, a 7% mortgage would only cost 5.04% after tax (7% times 28%=1.96%, or the deductible part of the mortgage. Subtract this from 7% to get 5.05%, the real after-tax cost). This means that you would need an after-tax return of just 5.04% in order to make the mortgage worthwhile. This 5.04% is much less than the average return on stocks, especially in the last couple of years.

Getting a math headache yet? Does anybody know how much cheaper a loan is if you're in an even higher tax bracket? Anybody? Anybody? Bueler?

If you are in the 39% bracket, the required investment return is even lower. The same 7% mortgage would result in an after-tax cost of 4.2%, requiring a mere 4.2% or greater stock market return to make a mortgage a better investment. Mortgages, although often viewed negatively, contain many benefits that should not be forgotten. First, you can maintain control of your investments and liquidate them as needed. On the other hand, if you sink you cash into a home equity, opening a home-equity line of credit will be required, which is a time-consuming process.

We've numbed you with the math. Do you believe us now, or do you want some more? We thought so.

---

4   This is subject to an overall limit on itemized deductions, which for couples occurs
    when adjusted gross income exceeds $124,500 for 1998.

ZOE AND TED

While their incomes as school teachers had only increased modestly over the last few years, Zoe and Ted had managed to increase their wealth by owning a home and a vacation home. Because both were located in hot real estate markets, their home and vacation home had gone up in value $350,000 and $50,000, respectively. Because the market was so strong, they decided to sell the house, and buy another home in another hot real estate market. In another two years, they plan to do the same thing all over again....all tax free!

How could they avoid taxes completely? Since 1997, married (filing jointly) homeowners who sell their principal residence can escape taxation on up to $500,000 in capital gains, or if single, up to $250,000. The rule holds, provided the person or couple used the home as their principal residence for at least two of the last five years. Sometimes called the "serial home strategy", this new law also provides a potential tax savings for owners of a second home, condo, vacation home, or even a rental home. For those homeowners whose property has increased in value and who now wish to sell their home to take advantage of the soaring real estate market, they can now have their cake and eat it too.

How can this law work for the married couple who wishes to sell both their home and their vacation home? First they sell the principal residence, paying no tax on capital gains of up to $500,000. Then they make a bona fide move into their vacation home where they live for two years, after which they may sell and, again, paying zero tax on up to the half million in capital gains. This is almost like tax-free income!

For those people who can afford to move every two years (the "serial" movers), this law could prove to be a real boon. Of course, the fact that the person must actually live in the residence for two years may keep some people form using it. But for those fortunate people who own property that has increased in value, as long as they live there for the requisite period, they can sell and begin the buying (and profiting) process all over again. The benefits should be greatest for young people starting a family who wish to move into a larger home, or older people who whish to move into smaller homes after retirement.

ED

Ed never really had much luck with anything. He has trouble holding a steady job, and his wives and pets always ran off. His house was just another example—by his estimate, it had gone down in value by nearly 20%. Fortunately, there was a silver lining: he had his property taxes reduced by $500 per year, based on a lower "assessed value". As an example of this, one homeowner in Colorado successfully challenged the assessment on his home to the tune of a $1200 per year savings on his annual property tax bill. Challenging one's assessed value is easier than you think. Many assessments are increasingly made through computer models rather than by an inspector who sees the house in person. The process makes errors more common, and review boards more sympathetic. The fact is, a computer will not see roof damage or any other type of damage that might lower the property's value.

While few people actually challenge their assessments, those who do usually win. Moreover, homeowners may challenge assessments based on a wide range of problems which may affect their home's value. Noises, a neighbor's messy property, and even bad smells have served as viable reasons to reassess a property's value. In addition, the homeowner does not need to go to the fight alone, since a growing number of tax representatives have begun to specialize in challenging assessments. To change the assessment, the taxpayer need only show that the assessment is "factually incorrect", or nor not in line with neighboring properties of similar characteristics.

Anyone who believes their assessment value is too high and wants to challenge it can use these tips. First, "Learn the Lingo"; learn the appraisal rules of your area before protesting. For example, local assessors may not count certain parts of your home as the square footage count. Second, always double-check records. Data collectors may not necessarily be well-trained and may be responsible for a large number of homes. Thus there is much room for error in this regard. Third, don't get emotional. A person is more likely to win on an assessment challenge if behavior is courteous and arguments are supported by convincing evidence. Don't lie about facts. Finally, document any flaws. Flaws can greatly reduce a home's estimated value. Estimated repair bills from at least two respected professionals in the repair business will help.

DOROTHY

While her husband Bob is at his full-time job, Dorothy sells cosmetics. She uses the extra bedroom of their house to store cosmetics, and to make calls to customers. Because the room qualifies as her "home office", she can deduct utilities, insurance, and depreciation attributed to the room. With depreciation alone, she manages to completely shelter her income from taxes!

If Dorothy had instead lived in an apartment, she would have been able to deduct rent attributable to the extra bedroom (instead of depreciation).

The deduction is made easier by a recent change in the tax rules. Beginning January 1, 1999, home offices meet a more relaxed definition of a principal place of business if:

The taxpayer uses the home office to conduct administrative or management activities of the business

The business has no other fixed location where the taxpayer conducts substantial administrative or management duties

The taxpayer uses the home office exclusively and on a regular basis for the business activity (Yep, move that foosball table out of there)

The home office is in a place for the convenience of the employer (if the taxpayer is an employee). To qualify as the principal place of business, a taxpayer must satisfy these requirements at all times.

If you plan to use the deduction, adequate records should be maintained to document the required regular and exclusive business use of the home office. A calendar or daily log of events and specific expenses, such as mileage, would be advisable. Special care should be allotted to situations involving employees. As with any planning issue, the non-tax implications should also be considered prior to using a home office. For example, local government zoning restrictions the possible intrusion of family members on business affairs, and limitations on homeowners' insurance coverage.

There are about 14 million home-based businesses that are operated by full-time self-employed workers, with 500,00 more being added every year. Only about 1.5 million of these businesses actually take advantage of home office deductions. By the year 2000, an estimated 11 million employees will spend at least part of their workweek in their home offices. Now, many people like Dorothy will be able to partly shelter their incomes. There's no place like home!

PAMELA

Pamela had worked as a nurse for a long time to save up enough to buy a vacation condo on the beach. Trouble was, she couldn't spend very much time there. So, she rented it out on a weekly basis to vacationers. Because she spent less than 14 days per year there (which was also less that 10% of the days the condo was rented out for its fair market value), she was able to tax deduct all costs related to it—insurance, maintenance, utilities, and depreciation. In her first year of ownership, she actually sheltered $1000 of her income as a nurse!

GIVE IT UP!

Renting out your vacation home can make both good business and tax sense. If you rent it out for 350 days or more for the year, you can deduct all costs related to it, including our friend depreciation. If you actually create a tax shelter out of it, that is, you expenses are more than your rental income, you can shelter your other income by up to $25,000 per year (less, if your income is above $100,000).

Income from rental properties is reported on Schedule E of your tax return. We show an example of this in the Appendix.

Now you've been involved with three tax tricks, which by FBI standards, makes you a serial tax-saver. You know you can't stop reading now….

Chapter 5

In Trusts We Trust

"In God we trust. All others we audit."

—Anonymous

This a well-known saying among CPAs , who are a little suspicious by nature. It is also reflective of our advice to clients. If you want to protect assets into the future with some degree of certainty, put them into a trust. It's kinda ironic that when you don't trust someone, you use a trust. Hey, we never said taxes made sense.

A trust is a separate legal entity in which a person can put virtually any type of asset. At some point or points in time, the trust distributes the assets back to either the person who put the assets in (the "grantor"), or to others who were named in the trust agreement ("beneficiaries"). Trusts are used for asset protection as well as for tax advantages, as our following wealthy client stories illustrate.

SAM

When we saw them walking arm-in-arm at the chic Century City Mall, we were stunned.

"Hey guys, come meet the new future Mrs. Sam!" he waved us over excitedly. The next future ex Mrs. Sam was a stunning tall blonde young enough to be Sam's granddaughter. We took bets on how much he would spend on her at the mall today. Maybe we could marry him for the day? (just kidding!).

As owner of one of the largest truck freight hauling companies in the country, Sam was a good businessman. His net worth was about $1 billion dollars. Unfortunately, he was not so smart in matters of the heart. His two previous marriages ended in divorce and millions of dollars in alimony and property settlements. Now getting serious with this new woman, his attorneys made him smarter. During one of his regularly-scheduled diving/fishing trips to Grand Cayman, on our advice, he stopped at an attorney's office, where within the day he established four trusts: one to hold most of his stock in his trucking empire, one for his real estate holdings (he owned a number of apartment buildings), and one for each of his two children (composed mainly of stocks and bonds). Within eight hours, about three-fourths of a billion of his net worth had "disappeared", Bermuda-triangle-style, from the prying eyes of the IRS and his future wife. Happy and relaxed, Sam enjoyed two weeks of sun before flying back home. Fortunately, his pane did not disappear in the Bermuda Triangle like his money.

"Off-shore" trusts are used regularly, by wealthy US individuals and big companies, to "hide assets", shelter income from taxes, or avoid regulations from the US government. They can be formed anywhere, but the best places for US individuals and firms tend to be in Caribbean island-nations like the Cayman Islands, the Netherlands Antilles (Aruba and Curaçao), and Bermuda.[5] Switzerland and Austria are also popular for

---

5   Many countries have their favorite off-shore havens. For example, the British, it is Jersey Island off the English coast.

hiding cash because of secrecy laws regarding bank accounts. However, unlike the Caribbean countries, there are no tax advantages to these European countries.

JEFFREY

He used to be one of our prize tax students. Somewhere along the line, he became tempted by the dark side. As a Miami lawyer to underworld figures, Jeffrey was well acquainted with laundering money. The idea was simple: every transaction was in cash, and never deposit more than $10,000 in cash in a bank during a short time period.[6] But the best way was to put cash into a bank where the country didn't give out names to anyone, or so-called "numbered accounts". When Jeffrey's law partner "disappeared"—Jeffrey was pretty sure he'd been killed by an unhappy client—he felt it was time to start putting money away in case he needed to "run". First, he formed a trust in Aruba, using a local lawyer there to do the paperwork. Next, he opened a numbered account in Aruba, transferring most of the $5 million in cash he had in his US accounts. The trust was the owner of the bank account, with Jeffrey named as its beneficiary. Happily, Jeffrey is still alive and well practicing law, but if he has to take a sudden "vacation", we know where he'll be.

MISTRUSTS

People often use trusts to try to hide assets. Take, for example, the 1998 U.S. District Court case of the U.S. versus Glenn D. Bell and Jeanette Bell. In this case, the defendants (the Bells) were high net worth individuals who tried to hide assets from creditors and the IRS through the use of trusts and a fraudulent tax shelter. The Bells owed the IRS approximately $3.7 million in taxes and interest. The government sought to foreclose against the property which was beneficially owned by the Bells. In determining that the Bells had beneficial ownership, the IRS noted that the property was transferred in and out of various trusts for a $0 price tag. The Bells owned two companies named stark management company and

6   Otherwise, US banks are required to report it to the IRS.

Nassau Life Insurance company. Glenn Bell had at least six trusts through the Nassau Insurance company. The Bells represented themselves in court and as the saying goes, the person who defends themselves in court has a fool for a client. Despite the elaborate setup, the judge saw through, and the Bells' lost the case.

One major reason that rich people set up trusts is to avoid estate or "death" taxes. The Federal government taxes the net wealth of rich people at a rate of up to 55% when they die, and many state governments heap on an additional tax. No wonder they spend millions on tax lawyers/CPAs to help them get out of it!

Basically, if rich people transfer ownership of their assets before death, they "bail" these assets out of their estates.[7] To get the assets out of their estates, but still retain control, one of the best ways is to put the assets into a trust. In Chapter Three, we talked about charitable lead and remainder trusts, where rich people put their art and cars, and thus get these assets out of their taxable estates.

ALL IN THE FAMILY

"Will you two stop fighting!" we yelled.

When we met them for dinner at the posh Spago, we thought this time would be different. But no, they even started fighting over *which table* to sit at. At this, like many Hollywood-type restaurants, some customer like to buy their own favorite table. Bob and Nina rejected our suggestion to try that for next time, because it probably gave them an excuse to fight over something.

Oddly, this chemistry helped their business. Both were successful psychiatrists, specializing in wealthy patients by gender—Bob got the male patients, Nina the females. And they could definitely empathize with their patients' hostilities toward the opposite sex.

The maitre de was already stuttering when he tried to calm them. Observing him pop a pill, Nina joked:

---

7   Of course, they can still be subject to a "gift tax", but that's another topic!

"Our people are everywhere!". Especially in this town, we thought.

"Kids, stop the fighting and listen for a sec. We've got a good one for you—the FLP." we said. Like dogs hosed with water, they were temporarily distracted. Alert to the possibility they could just as easily turn on us (perhaps diagnosing and toying with our one or two emotional issues), we spoke quickly about the FLP plan.

A favorite tax-buster is the family limited partnership, or FLP. The basic idea is simple: the rich person forms a partnership (of course, with the help of a lawyer) then puts most, if not all, of his/her assets into the partnership. The other partners are family members who get a free interest in the partnership (or they pay very little). We have had many of our clients do this. Basically, we set it up so that the Bob and Nina's interests in the partnership were subject to a "minority interest discount." In effect, we can often get much of the rich person's assets to escape the estate tax through this and other methods!

I DEFECT!

Before the fall of the Soviet Union, this was the dream of many communist-block countries. Today, for tax nerds, the dream is the "intentionally defective grantor trust." Here's the tax trick for our rich clients. Our favorite example of this was Bobby, a country-western singer. Bobby put a bunch of his assets into a trust, which was formed by an attorney we had on retainer. As with most people, Bobby's assets were real estate (two apartment buildings and a small shopping mall) and stock in his own corporation. The trick is that Bobby retains complete control over the trust, and therefore of the assets. Because of a weird rule in taxes, the income was taxed to him every year, and not to the trust. But the assets escape the estate tax, and the rich person (in this case, Bobby) still has control. So for example, if Bobby gets mad at one of his kids, he can threaten to cut them out of the trust!

JOSE

We knew Jose before his salsa band became famous. When he made the big bucks with a record contracts (over $50 million in royalties), we were there to help him to shelter his taxes from Uncle Sam. (Since we like salsa and Jose, we would have helped him anyway.). Because he traveled from his LA home frequently for concerts (including to his native Cuba), there was always some risk. So, we set up a living trust for him (it's called a living trust because it's set up when the grantor—in this case, Jose—is still alive). Basically, it transferred all of his assets into a trust. So, if the unthinkable happened, none of his assets could be subject to probate. That is, a judge would not be required to decide "who gets what". When probate happens, lawyers get a big fee, and it can take years to sort it out! But if there is a living trust, probate is avoided (along with the lawyer fees), and assets get to the heirs immediately.

Part of the arrangement was that if there were a medical emergency, Jose's wife would make a decision. If there was little or no chance of him recovering from some fatal condition, she could "pull the plug". As a proud man, that was the way he wanted it to be. His brother Carlos was the trustee of the living trust (we also set up a living trust for Carlos, with Jose as trustee). If the unexpected happened, Carlos would decide day-to-day medical emergencies, and do day-to day management of Jose's assets.

KATHLEEN

We had her set up a "trust for minors". As a recording artist, she established a trust for her two kids, Colleen and Sean. She put $1 million in each of the two trusts. The earnings on the trusts accumulated for college funds for the kids. She retained control of the assets, in case she wanted to have the trust put them in different investments. And, her kids' college was all but paid !

If you like these rich people's styles, then read on about how you can put trusts to work for you. You can set up living trusts, trusts for minors, and educational trusts *just like them*. In fact, we recommend it! Although there are kits you can buy to set up a trust, we recommend spending the extra few bucks and have a qualified attorney draft the agreements for you.

The next few examples of some additional tax tricks, which the non-wealthy have used, that you may want to try.

DOUG

At age 40, the last thing Doug should have been worried about was dying. But, truth be told, there was some family history of early heart attacks, so he wanted to be careful. In addition to his regular visits to his cardiologist, he took financial precautions, too. He bought a $1 million life insurance policy on himself , with the beneficiary being a trust he set up. That's right: he set up a life insurance trust, the sole purpose of which was to pay the premiums on his policy and, at his death collect the proceeds, and distribute the proceeds over time to his two daughters. His two daughters, Lisa and Jenny, were 8 and 10, respectively, and lived with his ex-wife. By using the plan, he would be able to support his daughters without worrying about his ex using the proceeds. And best of all, everything was completely tax free.

FAMILY EDUCATION AT A SUBSIDIZED PRICE

There are a number of tax breaks which anyone can use which, even though you don't need a trust to use some of them, as professors, we felt it was our duty to clue you in on.

Hope Credit For Higher Education

The Hope credit stand for "Hope and Opportunity for Post-secondary Education". It was established in 1997 by the Clinton administration. The "hope" credit is applicable to 1998 and later years. The maximum deduction is $1500 for students in their first two years of college or other qualified schools. Whoever qualifies for the deduction gets to take it for the first $1000 of tuition, and then they receive half of the second $100 (or $50). Parents are allowed to deduct this amount for each child they have. Therefor, if the parents have three children, the maximum credit they are allowed is $4500. In order to be eligible for the credit, a student must be enrolled half-time for at least one semester or quarter during the year. The disadvantage of this credit is that it phases out (for joint returns) starting at $80,000 and is completely phased out at income of $100,000. The adjusted gross income maximum obviously limits the use of the Hope credit for higher wage-earners.

Lifetime Learning Credit

The lifetime learning credit has fewer restrictions than the Hope credit. A student may be in any year of college, and a student does not have to be full or part time to qualify. For example, if one feels like taking a single computer course to brush up their skills, taking only one course may qualify for the deduction. As with the Hope credit, the deduction begins phasing out at $80,000 of income and completely phases out at $100,000 of adjusted gross income. Unlike the Hope credit, there is only a $1000 limit, regardless of many children are attending college. The lifetime learning credit offers a 20% tax cut on the first $5000 of tuition. Thus, the maximum tax cut for one year is $1000. The lifetime learning credit is applicable after June 30, 1998. The article suggests that eligible students may want to use the credit for the first couple of years of college and then use the lifetime learning credit for their junior and senior years since it offers a lower tax cut. A family may only sue one credit at a time for the same child. In other words, a student cannot qualify for the Hope credit and the lifetime learning credit simultaneously.

Educational IRA

The educational IRA is similar to a retirement IRA account, except that the accumulated amounts are used during a child's years in college rather than at retirement. One is allowed to put $500 per year into the account. The tax deduction must be made by the end of the year. No tax deduction is provided for the amount put into the account each year. Nonetheless, later deductions are tax free so long as the money is used for tuition, books, or room and board. The drawbacks of this program is that once the one's adjusted gross income on a joint return exceeds $150,000 (or $95,0000 when filing a single return), the yearly amount the yearly amount that one can put into the account (i.e., $500) is reduced. At the time the money is withdrawn, the amount of adjusted gross income does not matter. Therefore, a family can make over $150,000 at the time of the withdrawal and not be penalized. Since only small deposits may be made any one year, the educational IRA should be started early in order to beneficial for the future college student. The education IRA may become more useful in the future because Congress is considering raising the amount one can deposit each year.

Golden State Scholarshare Trust

As if those Californians don't have enough with great weather and beaches and all, there is now a brand new education tax break for Californians. The program is set up so that parents, regardless of their income level, will be able to set up money in a trust for their children's college education that will be taxed upon withdrawal at the students' seemingly lower tax rate. The money may be applied towards tuition, room and board, and books at all accredited schools in the United States. Accounts will began opening in July 1999. This year, it is expected that 70,000 accounts will be opened and 50,000 are expected to exist by 2008. The investments will be managed by TIAA-CREF of New York. There is no limit to the amount of income that may be deposited each year or that may be in the account at any one time. In addition, a family may begin saving for any accredited college at any time they wish. As long as the student is in a lower tax bracket than the parents, then the family will save money. Any excess money left in the account after the child finishes college may be applied towards a graduate degree or to the next child's college education.

Although families may start an account regardless of their income level there are some drawbacks to the program. First, the money in the account is invested rather conservatively and the expected rate of return is only between 7 and 9 per cent. As the child gets closer to entering college, the risk of investments will decrease in order to keep the student's money safe. Another drawback is that money withdrawn by the parents or money that is not used for a qualified education purpose is penalized at about 10% of the earnings. Savvy investors may be disappointed since they do not control how the money is invested and since there is a low return.

A positive aspect of the plan is that the parents still retain control over the money. Therefore, if they feel their child will waste the money, they may transfer the use of the account to another one of their children or just close the trust. Apparently, parents who establish other trust funds are concerned that when their child turns either 18 or 21 (depending on the specifications of the trust) they will spend all the money. The plan prevents this from happening by keeping control with the donor.

Education is becoming increasingly more important. Lawmakers have realized this trend and are making it easier for all students to attend colleges and universities by providing tax savings under qualified programs. The newest program for California, the Golden State Scholarshare, will be especially useful for middle class to upper middle class families to a good school but cannot afford the high cost. Hopefully, this bell-weather program will encourage other states to adopt similar programs.

HOW TO MAKE A DENT IN TUITION BILLS THROUGH UNIFORM GIFTS OR TRANSFERS TO MINORS ACT!

Next to buying a home, college tuition is most people's largest expense. *Our advice is don't have kids. Raise Labrador Retrievers in the garage. Just kidding.* While tuition bills can be staggering, starting to save early, and using some smart tax and financial aid strategies can lessen the impact of those bills when they do start coming. *Then those tears you shed during "Pomp and Circumstance" will be out of pride rather than financial pain. (Note: before you decide on the Labs in the garage option, you should know they don't play "Pomp and Circumstance" at the obedience school graduation!)*

There are several different tools you can use to save for college costs in tax advantaged ways. Perhaps the most common such tool is the Uniform Gifts or Transfers to Minors Act (UGMA/UTMA) account. This account can be set up without any start up cost. The earnings on this account are taxable to the child, (with the exception noted below) which is an advantage if the parents are at a high marginal tax rate.

There is a down side to the UGMA/UTMA account however. One disadvantage is that income in excess of $1,200 a year that is earned in the account of a child who is younger than 14 years old...is taxed at the parent's higher income tax rate. (Of course the first $1,400, $600 is sheltered by the child's personal exemption and the next $600 is taxed at a 15%.) In addition, the funds in the UGMA/UTMA account are available to the child at age 18 or 21 (depending on the state)…and the child may decide that a sports car or new wardrobe is much more important than the college tuition bills.

If you do not want to let your child have access to the account at age 18 or 21, you can set up a trust to pay for the child's education. Trusts do cost money to set up, but they do let you control how the money is spent.

One popular form of such a trust is the "Crummy Power" trust, where parents relinquish their rights to the money, which is managed by a Trustee. If funds are left over after college bills are paid, the money remaining can be given to the child at a later age. If the child does not attend college, the funds can be paid out as directed by the trust document.

The downside of creating a trust for college funds is that the trusts cost money to set up and to administer on an annual basis. In addition, when a trust fund accumulates the annual income, the income tax brackets are very compressed, and the child can be paying at a high bracket very quickly. The 15% bracket applies to income under $1,500. By the time income reaches $7,500, the tax rate is 39.6%.

There are other, non related considerations when saving for college tuition. One such consideration is the age of the child and the type of investments selected.

Prospective college students should also make themselves aware of any scholarships offered by their parents' employers, or their *own* employer if they are able to work during college or graduate school.

Finally, many scholarship programs assume that all the money saves in a child's name is available to pay for college. A smaller percentage of parents' money is counted. So, for people with incomes of less than $100,000, tax savings realized by making a transfer to the child may be less than the scholarships that the child might have otherwise been entitled to…if the money is save by the parent instead.

Obviously there are many options to consider in this area. Don't flounder and make a costly mistake, or do nothing, and be sorry later. Don't try to guess when making the wrong guess could cost you!

Planning for college is serious business, and needs serious attention.

Kids can't work at the hamburger joint like we did, and pay for school with that money. It takes a combined effort from you, your kids, their school, and a tax planner!

If you would like to see how to report income from trusts on your taxes, there is an example in the Appendix.

Already, four tax tricks up your sleeve, but you want more, don't you? You bad, bad, taxpayer you…. As your enablers, we can only say "Please don't read us some more!"

Chapter 6

Tax Tricks for Stock Trading

We realized the stock market craze had reached a fever pitch at a school benefit for one of our kids. Of course, at the dinner table we were at, the conversation centered on our kids, how public schooling was going down the tubes, and inflated myths from our suffering (but better-educated) days as youths. But within half an hour, the conversation turned to the stock market.

"Did you guys see that Microsoft went up 20 today?" asked a mother. Most of them had.

"I'm going to short my biotechs and get back into internets!" exclaimed a father of four. And then it started: conversations about market momentum, new technology stocks, would the Fed raise interest rates, etc. Most of them had internet access to on-line stock trading, such as E-Trade. Their voices trembled with the excitement that only unbridled avarice can ignite. Kids? Whatever—let's talk-Dow Index!

"So, who made money this month?" One of us asked, knowing the answer. There was an eerie silence, then a mother of two mumbled:

"I made a little on a steel company. Bought it just before a merger announcement, sold a profit the next day." She looked at her mashed potatoes as if they were tea leaves ready to give up a secret". "Course, I lost a few bucks here and there on some other companies, but that's life", she continued.

Actually, most of the people we know have lost just about as much money day-trading (buying stocks for a short period of time, then selling them, sometimes within the same day). Although there are chat rooms, stock guru services, etc to help out, we need to realize that there are brokerage firms with thousands of analysts out there who we are competing with. So, if you decide to day trade, instead of the more traditional "buy and hold" strategy, let's be careful out there!

As everyone knows, the US stock market has been "hot" over the last few years. In fact, the return on stocks has greatly exceeded virtually every other type of investment over the last 20 years.

The icing on the cake is the many favorable tax rules for stocks. For one thing, there's the maximum tax rate of 20% (or 10%, if you're normally in the 15% tax bracket). But there are other, less well-known tax tricks which the rich use....

STAN

"Hey, watch where you're going!" came the shout from the driver on Rodeo Boulevard. That got our attention, because LA people are too cool to yell, usually giving a honk of feigned offense.

We looked in the direction of the yell, and it was Stan, all smiles behind the wheel of his new vintage 1938 Mercedes sedan. Yellow with gold trim, it actually had *curtains* in the back seat windows. The plate of his newest Benz read "IAMMNYMAN".

"Beauty!" we shouted as he disappeared onto Wilshire Boulevard. The car turned the heads of not-easily-impressed BH (that's local for Beverly Hills) crowd in their Ferraris, Porsches, and Jaguars. Stan collected Mercedes the same way a frat boy collected empty beer bottles. Each was a trophy to his manhood (that's the 90's way of showing it, for some). His socialite wife Laura tolerated the monument to Stuttgart in her garages, realizing these cars probably prevented a midlife crisis. In case you're wondering, we all drive small, inexpensive imports—we're secure with ourselves, we rationalize.

Stan's main job is managing money for wealthy individuals, corporations, and pension funds. His company manages close to $1 billion in funds per year, for which Stan receives one-half of one per cent of the managed assets. That's right, he makes about $5 million a year. He keeps clients because his returns on managed assets are typically about ¼% higher than the market. Not much, unless you multiply that by $1 billion! His main trick is to track stocks, then when it looks like the market will drop enough, to pull out of the stock market and put the money into cash (money market funds, etc). Then, when the timing is right, he goes back into the stock market..

Another trick is to pick the right mutual stock mutual funds to invest his client's money in. His tax tricks include selling mutual funds before they pay dividends—basically, turning regular taxable income (taxed to most of his clients at 36%) into capital gains (taxed at 20%), which increases the after-tax returns to his clients by 33-1/3%. To his clients, he is a hero.

RICHARD

Richard is a venture capitalist. That is, he sniffs out promising startup companies, and loans them money, in return for ownership interest in the company's stock. If the company succeeds, and goes public at a high stock price, Richard can make back up to 20 times his investment. His specialty is internet companies. He has an important tax trick up his sleeve as well:

making sure the company qualifies as "small business stock." Using this rule, 50% of any gain he makes on each company he invests in is tax-free.

LISA

Lisa is a successful tax attorney, and as a partner in a large law firm, she makes in excess of $1 million per year. On the side, she drafts documents which put together startup companies. Instead of charging a fee for her work, she simply takes back stock ownership in the companies. Her risk is smaller because of a tax rule called "Section 1244 stock". Under this provision, she and her husband can tax deduct the entire amount of her stock investment if it tanks, up to a maximum of $100,000. If we compare this to the normal tax rules which limit tax deductions to $3000 per year, it is almost like having an insurance policy.

JIM

Jim quit his full-time job as a trader for one of the major stock brokerage firms to strike out on his own. Now, he is a day trader, making money on small movements in stock prices every day. He runs his $2 million a year empire out of his house, using one of the four bedrooms in his home for the business. Because it is a legitimate business, Jim can tax deduct all expenses related to it—utilities, insurance, depreciation (on the bedroom, its furniture, and equipment). Any magazines and journals which might help his investing are tax deductible. Any trips he takes which provide training which is also helpful can be deducted. He spent a week in Hawaii at an investment conference. Also, any losses he has on trades are fully deductible; for casual investors like you and me, such losses may be deductible up to $3000 per year.

ALEX AND MARCIE

This couple runs a successful advertising agency, grossing over $20 million per year. Although they have a staff of about 100, they own the operation as equal partners in a partnership. Their two children earn their allowance by doing miscellaneous tasks around the office—typing, photography, etc. As "employees" of the operation, the kids' wages are tax deductible. The couple has another partnership in which their children are partners. The partnership owns investments, primarily in stocks. Because the kids own 52%, and the parents each own 28%, each parent is considered to be a minority owner. As such, the value of the parents' interests is lower than its real value due to a "minority discount". This discount will eventually save them about $1 million in estate taxes.

MARKET MAVENS

*Disney CEO Michael Eisner knows how to save taxes. Recently, before tax rates were due to go up in January, he exercised millions of dollars in stock options, so he would have the income taxed at a lower tax rate!

*Bill Gates is officially the richest man in the world. His estimated net worth is over $ one billion, comprised primarily of stock in Microsoft.

*Warren Buffet is the chairman of Berkshire Hathaway corporation. He is one of the wealthiest men in the world. Essentially, he is a buyer and seller of companies, with his acquired companies becoming subsidiaries of Berkshire Hathaway. If you buy stock in his company, you are essentially investing with him in his stock picks.

*Much more money may be associated with initial public offerings than we might imagine. When a firm goes public, its stock price is typically based on earnings expectations, which are based on the company's past earnings. Lately, this "rule of thumb" has been completely shattered by internet IPOs, which are so new, they only have ideas to sell—no earnings or assets! So, their initial stock price is often based on the number of engineers or computer scientists they employ.

*George Soros is also one of the wealthiest men in the world. He speculates, or bets on foreign currency. For example, if he thinks the value of the Italian Lira will go up soon, he buys millions (perhaps billions) worth of Lira with US dollars. When the Lira goes up, he sells them at a profit. His investment firms are located in the Caribbean, where taxes and regulation are minimal.

OK, what makes these rich guys and gals tick? When they already have more money than entire African countries, why pursue more? There's no single answer. Some of the self-made millionaires are releasing years of frustration; nerds, little guys, or somehow outcasts in school, they're now proving themselves. Maybe they're secretly plotting to hire their high school enemies, then systematically torture them with depantsings, random hecklings over the PA system, or assigning them accounting jobs.

Most, however, are individuals who thrive on challenge. They get up in the morning not thinking about how they can spend the new day's earnings, but how they can succeed at something interesting that day. The money's not the primary thing. So, why don't you befriend one of these individuals and trade adulation for some of their bucks? OK, that was lame. But here are some tax ways you can imitate them in the market.

SAMMY

Sammy was a shrewd trader. As a physician's assistant (P.A.), he saved up enough that he had cash he could "play with". Also, many of the doctors he worked with dabbled in the stock market, so he was always getting tips from them. One practice he put to regular use was selling stocks pre-dividend. Here's how it works. After his companies announced their upcoming dividends, the stock's price would increase. Instead of holding onto the stock, collecting the dividend, and paying taxes at his normal 36% tax rate, he would sell the stock for its higher price, but only pay the 20% capital gains tax rate. The tax savings, and the sales proceeds, he would then reinvest in a new company's stock. He hoped to have saved a million dollars by the time he retired!

KATHERINE

As a single mom, Katherine had to work two jobs as a waitress to make ends meet. Luckily, after her divorce, she was left with a $30,000 nest egg form the sale of their house. $10,000 of this was in a safe money market account, but the rest she invested in relatively safe utility company stocks. With investments in 20 companies, she tracked her stocks' performance daily in the Wall Street Journal. When she felt the stock was going no higher in the near future, she sold, usually at a gain. Occasionally, however, some of her stocks "tanked", and she would sell them at a loss. As with much in life, timing is everything. She soon learned to sell loss stocks in the same years as gains. The reason: the tax law allows a maximum loss of $3000 per year, unless there are gains to offset them with. Also, by timing gains with losses, she reduced her taxes on gains. All tolled, she paid very little in taxes on her investments.

DARRYL

Darryl was a recovering day trader. As a cashier at a supermarket, he made enough (union-based) wages to be comfortable. But, after losing $20,000 in day trading last year, we advised him to stick to a more conservative "buy and hold" strategy. When he did sell a stock, he made sure he had owned it for at least a year and a day. The reason: when held for this time, it became a "long-term capital gain", which was taxed at a maximum tax rate of 20%. If held less than a year, his normal 28% rate would apply. Over the years, by reinvesting this 8% savings, his retirement nest egg continued to grow.

"Paper or plastic? Me, I recommend the more reliable, old fashioned paper. Plastic looks pretty sexy, but don't ever trust it a second. It'll just tear your fingernails out and leave you! " he ranted last time we saw him at the supermarket. Yikes! We never intended to have this kind of effect.

SUSAN

There were few people with a bigger heart than Susan. She worked as a volunteer for charity events, and was constantly giving money to friends and relatives. One day, her new boyfriend came to her to "borrow" $4000 to start up a tanning salon business.

"Although I've only known him three weeks, don't you sometimes feel that you've known someone before?" She said. Based on her previous picks, we guessed she was right: he was just like all her other losers, with a little Ted Bundy thrown in.

On our advice, she structured it as a "real" loan with an 8% interest rate, to be paid back over 5 years. Within 6 months, her boyfriend's business folded, and he announced he could not pay her back. Turns out he used most of it for back child support on his previous three marriages.

Because the loan was considered a "non-business bad debt" by the tax code, she could tax deduct $3000 of the loan this year, and the remaining $1000 next year.

The boyfriend's gone now...so it could've been worse.

WHEN GOOD LOANS GO BAD

Here's some helpful hints on loans which go bad, and how you can tax deduct them....

*If you regularly make loans, then any loans are completely tax deductible, with no limit. The tax code calls this a "business bad debt".

*If you're not in the business of making loans, like Susan, bad loans are "non-business bad debts". Deductible as short term capital losses, the maximum deduction is $3000 per year.[8]

*If the loan does not look like a real loan to the IRS (say, no interest rate), it's considered a gift. And it's non-deductible.

*Any loans to relatives are suspect by the IRS, and are usually non-deductible. *Sorry Uncle Lou, you'll have to borrow the money for your combination laundromat/mud-wrestling bar somewhere else.*

A KILLER DEAL

One exception to the IRS' disallowance of bad debt deductions involved the 1999 Tax Court case of Barr, et al v. Commissioner. In 1990, Jeffrey Barr loaned his brother Stephen $100,000 in a loan with a structured interest payment of 13%. Also, the loan had to be paid off in 18 months. Jeffrey's father, Meyer, bought the note from Jeffrey because it was an "attractive investment" to him as a professional investor. Meyer and his son Stephen were estranged at the time. Soon, trouble began. Stephen, whose business sold meats to Chinese restaurants, allegedly got in trouble with the Chinese Mafia. Next, Stephen was indicted for the murder of his business partner, and his legal defense left him penniless.

---

8 If a person has any capital gains for the year, a non-business bad debt can be deducted to the extent of the gain.

When he could not repay the loan to his father, the tax court allowed the deduction as a non-business bad debt.

MIKE

As a middle manager in a manufacturing firm, Mike made sure to invest his money wisely. Most of it was in the stock market, which he followed daily. One day a friend came to him with a movie script, which he wanted to produce. But, he needed financial backing, to the tune of $100,000.

"You realize most of these fail?" we warned.

"Uuuuhhhh.. but I really love movies" He whined. "Besides, he'll give a card that says 'Producer', and chicks will dig it" he pleaded.

Mike argued that many successful hits came from such independent producers(for example, Blair Witch Project). So, he took the plunge, investing $20,000 with four other people who did the same. On our advice, they organized the venture as an "S corporation", and elected to have the stock treated as "Section 1244 stock". As it turned out, no one bought the rights to the movie, so Mike lost his investment. But there were two silver linings. First, the tax break: by electing sec. 1244, his entire $20,000 was tax deductible, which resulted in a tax refund of almost $8,000.[9] Second, his friend's second movie was bought by a major studio for $1 million, and he gave Mike a new BMW to show his gratitude!

GIMME SHELTER

Investment banking firms, tax lawyers, and national CPA firms are constantly coming up with new "products" involving stocks and bonds, which are essentially tax shelters. Here are some of the investments they have cooked up in the past:

*Shorting against the box. Family members of the Estee Lauder company saved so much taxes on this, that Congress finally outlawed it. Here,

9 If you invest in the stock of a qualified small business company which elects Section 1244, you can automatically deduct losses up to $50,00 ($100,000 if you file a joint return).

family members essentially "shorted" their stock by borrowing another family member's stock, then issuing it in a public stock offering. Because issuing stock in a public offering is tax free, this scheme allowed people to sell stock without paying taxes.

*Foreign hybrid products. Although the US tax code has cracked down on many stock/bond tax shelters, the inventors of such ideas simply sell the ideas to foreign investors, whose governments are less sophisticated than the US. One popular investment is the hybrid product—or a hybrid between stocks and bonds. Here, a company sells "stock" to a European investor(s), which is really a bond since it pays interest. Since many European countries do not tax dividends, the payments the investor(s) receive are tax free, and the paying corporation gets a tax deduction for "interest" expense.

PUTTING YOUR EX'S STOCK WHERE THE SUN DON'T SHINE

When a couple gets divorced, there is no tax to either on splitting up the property. This can actually provide unexpected results when a couple co-owns a corporation, as in the 1999 US Tax Court case of Linda Craven v. US. Because the divorce decree required her to sell her stock back to the corporation (in reality, back to her husband), she essentially sold her stock tax free. On the other hand, her ex husband paid taxes on a "dividend" in the process!

Gains and losses on stocks, bonds, and bad debts are reported on Schedule D of your form 1040. If you'd like to see an example of this on your taxes, there's one in the Appendix.

Feeling pretty good about now, aren't you? Five tax tricks up your sleeve, and they haven't caused weight gain, addiction, or any other nasty side effects. Go ahead with the next one…you're not being a pig.

Chapter 7

Stock Options for Everyone

Like playing the Lotto? Really dig corporate office pools? Then employee stock options may be for you. First, let's tease you with stories of the big boys' stock option bonanzas.

We all know that presidents of really big companies get paid a lot. *What may surprise you is the magnitude of their compensation, which comes from stock options.* The table below reports some of this, for 1996.[10]

10 From the Wall Street Journal, April 10, 1997.

STOCK OPTIONS FOR TOP EXECUTIVES

Name/Company	Total Compensation	Stock Option Gains
Wayne Sanders (Kimberly-Clark)	$7.7 mil.	$4.8 mil.
Lee Raymond (Exxon)	10.1 mil.	5.9 mil.
Drew Lewis (Union Pacific)	17.3 mil.	14.3 mil
John Amerman (Mattell)	20.4 mil	18.5 mil
Anthony O'Reilly (H.J. Heinz)	64.1 mil.	61.5 mil.
Stanford Weil (Travelers Group)	93.9 mil.	85.2 mil.

It's not just the corporate fat-cats getting in on the option action, either. Below are some athletes and entertainers who received generous options:[11]
*Michael Jordan, basketball player (various companies)
*Cal Ripken, Jr., baseball player (Oakley Sunglasses)
*Kent Steffes, volleyball player (Foothill 76ers)
*Dale Earnhardt, NASCAR driver (Action Performance, Inc.)
*Tiger Woods, golfer (Official All Star Café, Planet Hollywood)
*Greg Norman, golfer (Corbra Clubs)
*Jerry Seinfeld, entertainer (NBC)
*Bryant Gumbel, TB personality (CBS)

11 From April 7, 1997 article in the Wall Street Journal.

As an example, Greg Norman earned $40 million on a $2 million option when Cobra, Inc. went public, and was subsequently acquired by American Brands, Inc.

So, what are they? Employee stock options[12] are pieces of paper which give you the right (only if you want to) to purchase stock in your company at a fixed price. Let's say an executive gets 100 stock options which each allow him to buy a share of stock at $140 per share. Let's say the stock is selling on the stock market for $140 per share. If the stock price goes to, say, $150, then the options are said to be "in the money", and the executive can either trade them in to the company for stock, or else have the company pay him the $10 per share "spread". If the company's stock never goes above $150, the options are said to be "underwater", and while the employee gains nothing, he loses nothing either.

KATHLEEN

Known as a "hard charger" in the telecommunications industry, Kathleen moved up to vice president of marketing at her company. To us, she was the kind of kick-butt chick who we secretly called Shira, the phone warrior. With compensation of almost $1 million annually (comprised partly of bonuses), she was satisfied, but bored. The glass ceiling in her huge corporation was not going to allow her to progress to CEO in the foreseeable future. When the offer came to be president of a startup cellular phone company, she jumped at the chance. The salary was only $100,000 per year, but she was given an option to buy 100,000 shares of the company's stock for $1 per share. The company was privately owned by its founder, an electrical engineer with little business knowledge. Since the company had no profits, the stock was essentially worthless. Within two years, Kathleen had made the company hugely successful. When its 1

12 You can actually buy non-employee stock options, just like stock, on the market. These are basically bets that the price of a company's stock will either go up or down. For a minimal amount (less than the cost of the stock itself), you can either make or lose a huge amount of money. Unless you have a lot of expertise in this area, or are a masochist, we recommend you stay clear of them!

million shares of stock went public, they sold for $150 per share. She cashed in her options, sold the stock, and made a $14.9 million profit! Of course, Kathleen had to pay taxes on the profits at the 36% tax rate. Oops, we fumbled! A small price to pay for such a bundle! There are ways to actually reap some tax benefits as well, as told in the next story.

SHUPING

As a recent immigrant to the US from Asia, Shuping embodies the best of her culture—hard working, intelligent, and persistent. After getting her MBA , she considered a job at an import business for $120,000 plus stock options. The stock options were "qualified stock options", which meant that there was no tax to her when she exercised them.

Before accepting the offer, we had a conversation over some delicious dim sum at a Chinatown restaurant. She had a competing offer from an established company for more money, but no stock options. The conversation centered on options.

"Do you like to take risks?" We asked.

"I'm eating this, aren't I?" she replied.

She was surgically removing the eyes and brain from a fish head entrée. There it was, staring up with surprise. Where did the edible part of this fellow end up, we wondered?

"Go for it", we said. We were actually referring to the entrée, but we later found out she interpreted the comment as about the job. Turned out well, anyway. The company stock later went up in value, she exercised her options, all tax free. A little over a year later, she sold the stock for a tidy profit, which was taxed at the 20% tax rate, well below her regular tax rate of 36%!

For executives, qualified stock options are a better deal, since there is no tax on exercise—only on the sale of the stock. The story is different for companies, however. Since they can tax deduct non-qualified options, but can't deduct qualified options, they prefer the former. So, we advise executive clients to negotiate with their companies on the types of options.

KEN

Son of a former motion picture executive, Ken's skills in picking "winner" movies was legendary in the business. Courted by many other motion picture companies, when Ken's contract was up for renewal, he knew he had market power, so he asked for, and received, a $10 million per year cash salary. As for options, he was able to receive $5 million worth by agreeing to get non-qualified options. Essentially, the tax savings that the company got by having tax-deductible options, was partly passed on to him through more options.

Encouraged by the success of Slingblade, Ken purchased the rights to several independent films he saw at the Sundance Film Festival. One turned out to be an incredible hit. After seeing it, we had to call. We can't tell you the name of this movie, because you'd instantly I.D. the studio, and Ken.

"Great film, Ken!" We had to call. There was as much pride as if Ken were one of our own kids.

"Thanks, guys. I'm amped and I think this'll set the industry on its ear!" Ken was almost shouting with excitement, quoting a review in one of the industry "trades".

"Ken, have you been watching FNN? Your company's stock just went up 18%. Buddy, your options are so in the money. You're up...$2 million today!" Gushing pride again, we were.

"Whatever. Come down to the studio....I want your take on a class project these kids from NYU made..."

Artists. Thank goodness for them.

One reason big companies love options is that they're "off the financials". That is, instead of showing up on their public financial statements as an expense (which reduces earnings) or on their balance sheets as a debt, they are often buried in a footnote in the company's financial statements. For practical purpose, they are invisible and keep the company's stock price high. Aw yeah.... more American stealth technology.

RAUL

"Hey fellas, we're about to go public, and need some advice" asked Raul. We kept in touch with our former student, who left a lucrative job with a major CPA firm to become chief financial officer (CFO) with an upstart company that was integrating the internet with cable tv. Really cool stuff.

"Beg your people to take options, instead of salary. It will increase earnings by $1 million... and get you guys maybe $1 million more on the IPO, depending on the I-bankers." The success of the initial public offering (IPO) depended much on the investment bankers who, if the company made them happy (with booze and girls...sorta kidding) impressed them and thus the investors. We were pretty jealous of I-bankers who got paid on a commission basis (a per cent of the IPO), and could easily make $1 million per year. Many retired at 40, rich, and also in rehab.

Most of the employees did agree on options, and the IPO fetched a whopping $40 million. You'll see their product on your cable provider soon...look for it...

Kinda dig these rich people's styles? Check out how you can copy them....

First, on how to get stock options. If you're not an "O" (CEO, CFO, BMFO, etc, you get it) it's probably more likely going to happen if you hook up with a startup company. It used to be that technology-related companies did this (bio-techs, hi-techs, etc). Now, a buncha new companies are "turned on" to the use of options.

Now, if you're close to collecting your pension from Bigco, we're certainly not recommending you quit to join a startup that may tank. But, if you're young at heart (read: love gambles), this may be the way to go.

KATE

At age 40, Kate should've been very conservative. If she hadn't been recently dumped by her jerk-of-a-husband for a twenty-something secretary, left to support three wonderful kids, this may've been the case. But now, re-entering the workforce after a 20 year absence, she was willing to take a chance. Through an old friend, she learned of an upstart company which made computer games. Although she could be an executive secretary for $40,000 at a law firm, she looked ahead, and saw the possibilities in this $20,000 per year job, plus options in the company' stock.

At the interview with the company's founder, a Caltech graduate almost half her age, he began:

"What makes you think you can add value to our company?"

"Young poop." She thought. But, a smart one. She accepted the offer. Two years later the company went public, she exercised her options, and made a $300,000 profit. A month later, her ex called for a reconciliation.

"Bug off." She told him, hanging up. With a new house and her children well provided for, she had little tolerance for depending on an unreliable person.

PETER

Peter had just gotten divorced (actually a very messy divorce) and was having a difficult time making the transition to being a bachelor. At 44 years old, getting into the dating scene was kind of tough.

Peter had always been a very strong person who never let anything get him down. In fact, he liked challenges, and used to thrive in any situation where he had to face a challenge…and rise to the occasion. Getting divorced from his wife Cindy however, was something quite different. They had been married for over 20 years, (they met in college) and had three children. One of whom was a junior in college, and doing real well as a volleyball player. The other two children were finishing up high school. All three were what you would basically describe as good kids.

When Cindy announced that she was leaving Peter, (actually hit him over the head with a sledge hammer would be a better description), he was devastated. That was over a year ago, and when he came in to see us, his divorce had just been finalized. In fact, not everything in Peter's life was going badly. His financial situation wasn't too at all. You see, he had started working for this company when he had just left college, and they were just a small start up operation. Now they have over 5,000 employees, offices all over the United States and in three foreign countries, and he was near the top of their "food chain."

When he first started working for the company, Peter was given the choice of taking some raises in the form of current salary or, taking stock options in the Company (betting on the Company's future).

At that time Peter made what is now easily seen as the wise choice. He chose the stock options instead of the raises. These were given to him at little or no cost. By the time Peter came in to see us, the value of the stock options was well over $1 million dollars—$1,356,000 to be exact!

Because Peter's divorce had finalized before he came in to see us, we didn't feel too good about pointing out the way his assets had been split up during his divorce was certainly to his disadvantage. He had been using an accountant (a friend that he had gone to college with) to handle most of his divorce issues. He also used an attorney who didn't really specialize in complicated tax issues.

You see, Peter was not only given the emotional shaft by Cindy. Her attorneys and accountants did an excellent job of making sure that Cindy's tax situation, after the split, left Peter holding the bag for all kinds of income taxes due. Taxes which should have probably been split 50/50…as opposed to Peter bearing the whole burden.

If he had known then, what he knows now after working with us, he wouldn't have had those kinds of problems. In fact, people getting divorced should always understand that there are many, many tax issues that can be resolved, and can end up being quite fair…or can end up being quite unfair, as in this case. Most people don't understand how complicated this stuff is, and how many ways it can be worked out.

In Peter's case, he got the worst end of the deal. Now here's the problem with the stock options. Peter has $1,356,000[+] in stock options, and he had considered exercising them to get some money (he suddenly finds himself in need of money for some strange reason).

In order to do that, the tax consequences would've been as follows:

If Peter would exercise the options and sell them, he would owe approximately $596,0000 in income taxes. Yes—you read that right!

$596,000 in income taxes! In fact, if he hadn't come in to see us, he would have been nailed to the wall with these taxes.

We, of course, immediately told him to stop. We wanted to understand his reasons for selling these options and to take a look at his whole financial situation. We suggested that he do a plan, so that he could take stock of his whole situation (no pun intended) and see just what he needs to do in all financial areas…and then decided the best thing to do with these options, in conjunction with everything else.

As it turned out, he didn't really have any kind of a plan. He was just going to exercise these options, because he felt that the company had reached its potential. In fact, he was thinking about leaving the company to try to go into business for himself.

Well, we put a plan together with Peter, and we were able to show him a lot of things. We showed him things like how to:

Sell part, or all of the stock…*without paying any income taxes at all!* (Totally legally, of course!)

Receive income from the sale stock, when he wants, and only when he wants! (Thereby deferring taxes on income he doesn't need right now.)

Seven ways to get legal tax deductions for things he was doing before without getting any deductions! (His accountant didn't tell him any of this!)

Protect his assets, so no one would have much of a chance to ever get at his wealth in any kind of lawsuit or legal action!

So, as you see, Peter was able to save almost $600,000 in income taxes that he otherwise would have wasted. Peter is able to maintain the use of those assets for the rest of his life, and he has a plan for himself so that he can move into the future, confident and with a solid foundation underneath him!

No matter what Peter does, he will be okay. Except for the hole that the sledgehammer left in his heart…

If you want to see how to report stock options on your taxes, we have an example in the Appendix.

One last thing on employee stock options. Don't confuse them with an Employee Stock Option Plan, or ESOP. This is actually a type of retirement plan your company can offer. Instead of investing your future retirement money in general stock and bond funds, the plan invests in your own company's stock. This can be a good deal if you expect your company to keep growing or becoming more profitable. Otherwise, it's probably better to stick for the more typical retirement plans.

If you'd like to see an example of how to report stock options for tax purposes, there's one in the Appendix.

OK, one more tax trick and your Jedi training will be complete.

Chapter 8

Retirement, Courtesy of Uncle Sam

When we're not worrying we're too fat, every American is worried that they will not have enough money to retire on. And, what about our future special needs: Denny's specials, a little Friday bingo action, annual RV pilgrimages to warm places. We all suspect that Social Security will be underfunded. We can only hope that any personal savings we have—perhaps set up through a company pension account, or if we are lucky, through our own IRA plans or 401k's—will be enough to do the trick.

Wealthy people don't need to worry about such problems. They can afford liposuction. And, they have some very creative tax tricks at their disposal to help enhance their retirement wealth, as we discuss in the next few pages.

MARK

Mark was the new breed of Chief Executive Officer (CEO): physically fit, juice-drinking, non-smoking, and computer-literate. No balding, cigar-chomping fat cat image for him, man. He hated Mr. Spacely from the Jetsons as a kid. Full of animal spirits and ego, he demanded and got a generous compensation package from his Fortune 100 employer: $3 million salary, $10 million bonus (in an average year), and stock options worth $6 million. Unfortunately, by law, the most that he and his company could sock away in his pension fund was limited to about $30,000— not nearly enough to keep him used to the lifestyle to which he had become accustomed. So, the company set up a so-called "non-qualified" pension plan. Instead of actually putting money into a pension account for him, the company simply set aside $1 million per year on its books, which earned fictitious interest, and would be paid to him in cash up retirement, or leaving the company. Since he didn't actually have any cash in hand, the amounts were not taxable to him until received. Best of all for the company, they didn't have to show these amounts on their financial statements, so shareholders had no idea of the real magnitude of Mark's compensation. Stealth technology!

Many top executives are now benefiting from such non-qualified plans. In general, all pension plans are under the eye of the Department of Labor, which provides limits for employer /employee contributions, rules on when employees must be covered, and rules which prohibit discrimination of plans in favor of any types of employees.

LIFESTYLES OF THE CEO

Because there is intense competition for CEO talent, many companies offer generous perquisites to their top executives. Since many of these bennies are taxable, companies often simply pay the executive an additional bonus to cover the CEOs tax costs of the bennies. Some other perquisites may surprise you:[13]

13 From David Rynecki and Gary Strauss, "Benefits of Being CEO: Companies Get Creative With Sky-High Pay, Perks" USA Today, June 15, 1998

*Don Tyson, who retired as Tyson Foods' CEO in 1991, got $235,000 for travel and entertainment in 1998, plus $164,000 to cover taxes on those perks. As Tyson chairman, he earns $700,000 a year, and owns Tyson stock worth $9.4 million.

*KMART paid $165,292 for CEO Floyd Hall's housing and living costs in 1997 at two residences in Michigan and New Jersey. He also earned $6 million.

*SunTrust Banks covered $100,000 in country club dues for CEO James Williams in his final year before retiring.

*Occidental Petroleum said it provided three senior executives personal use of corporate aircraft worth nearly $300,000.

SHEILA AND BEN

This couple owned a highly-successful PR firm in Los Angeles. They wanted to have some money set aside for the kids in case something happened to them. *DUUUHHH!!* Ben honestly believed that the more vodka martinis he had, the better he skippered his 42 foot sailboat. Wait, this gets better: he can't swim. And Sheila drove her gold Rolls Royce with minimal use of the brake pedal, especially when Nordstom's or Saks had a sale going on. So, they established a number of trusts for the kids, and also used a tax trick: they set up and Individual Retirement Account (IRA) for each of their two kids. Although they couldn't take a tax deduction for the annual $2000 contribution to each kid's IRA, the earnings from the IRAs (invested in the stock market) accumulated tax-free. To see how important this is, let's take a look at Adam, their 18 year old son. If Adam instead waited until age 25 to open an IRA, he would have $518,000 (assuming an 8% return) by age 65. By opening the account at age 18, he would have $905,000 at age 65. That's right, the extra 7 years is worth nearly $400,000.

DOCTOR TIM

Tim screamed into the phone "I worked my butt off and when I go, I don't want to give another cent to those rat b@#$&!^s."

A successful cosmetic surgeon in chic Newport Beach, Tim was a self-made millionaire and really hated the IRS.

The call kind of disturbed us, especially since Tim had just recently gone through his third divorce. Pretty average for, LA, actually. But bad for Tim's finances.

"Uh, Tim, you haven't purchased any firearms lately, have you? You know they're not tax-deductible…but tax planning is. So why don't you come by and let's see if we can't get you out estate taxes" we cooed in our best Dr. Frazier Crane voice.

We've all heard of death (or estate) taxes. Rich people spend a lot of time trying to avoid them; at a maximum tax rate of 55%, we can see why! The tax is on a person's net estate at death, which is basically the value of all assets owned, minus any debts owed, at the time of death. Unless your taxable estate is in excess of $650,000, there is no tax—that's why most of us don't worry about it. Rich people can get out of the tax through some simple techniques, like leaving assets to the surviving spouse, gifting assets to charity, etc. There are also a number of more sophisticated ways to avoid death taxes, some of which involve retirement accounts, as discussed next.

CARLOS

Carlos was your classic over-accumulator of wealth. Even though he was a successful venture capitalist (he loaned money to successful startup hi-tech companies), and his net worth was in excess of $100 million, he was still consumed with saving more money. He drove a 15 year old car, and lived in a one bedroom apartment. A self-proclaimed permanent bachelor, he planned to leave his estate to help the children in the poor South American village where he was raised. Of course, he used tax-advantaged retirement plans to their fullest. He set up a pension plan for his investment company, C-Tech. As sole shareholder and President, and only employee of C-Tech, the plan was set up to provide maximum benefits for himself. It contributed the legally maximum $30,000 per year to the plan, which the company tax deducted, and which accumulated tax free-over time. The plan invested in the same hi-tech companies that he did, and he expected that age 60 it would have accumulated another $10 million. Of course, he did not plan to use the money himself. The plan was that it would go to the village where he grew up upon his death, tax free. Because he set up a charitable organization (a private foundation) to help the village, the $10 million gift would be free of both income and estate taxes.

Carlos' example is not uncommon. Many people leave their money in their pension plans, IRAs, and 401ks until death, knowing that when their surviving spouse, children, or whoever takes the money out, it is free from both income and estate taxes.[14]

For professional athletes, careers are typically short, so the athlete needs to accumulate an enormous amount of wealth in a short period of time, in order to fund their early retirement. The following two stories illustrate two tax-savings ways of doing this.

DEON

As a professional boxer, Deon realized all two well that his pro career could likely last only 10 years or so. Further, there was always the possibility of serious injury which could retire him in a hurry. So, at our advice, he formed a Personal (or Professional) Service Corporation, or PSC. Doctors and Lawyers have used them for years, primarily for legal protection (if a client sues them, they can only sue for the corporation's assets, not the assets of the professional). But, there is a tax advantage too: since the corporation would pay taxes on his income at the 35% tax bracket, whereas he would pay at the 39.6% bracket, he would save 4.6% times his annual earnings of about $2 million, or about a quarter of a million in taxes. Of course, being organized as a corporation, he set up a generous pension plan for himself, as well as a *very necessary* medical and dental plan![15]

14 Of course, the IRS has figured out this strategy, too. As a result, for some retirement plans, there is a penalty excise tax if the person does not start taking distributions from the plan by age 70-1/2.

15 Before you set up a PSC, it's important to realize that any income must be paid directly to the corporation by agreement. That is, a boxer cannot sign a fight contract, then later tell the promoters to simply make out the check to his corporation. Instead, the contract should be between the promoter and the PSC.

MARCEL

After 10 years in professional hockey, Marcel knew that his career was coming to an end. Lately one morning, his aching knees reminded him. And, he wondered, how did he get that bruise on his *armpit*, anyway? So, on our advice, he rearranged his contract with his team for the next two years. Instead of receiving a performance bonus (based number of goals scored, minutes played, etc) at the end of each season, the bonuses would be deferred for three years in an interest-bearing account. Since he figured to be retired from hockey then and in a much lower tax bracket, this "deferred compensation" plan would save him substantial taxes, not to mention that he had some money salted away for retirement. Marcel has cross-checked the IRS into the boards.

Like how the rich people work the tax system for retirement and wealth accumulation? Then see how the average guy or gal can do the same....

LAURA

As a dental hygenist, Laura's $40,000 per year earnings provided her with a little extra money to invest. Her first thought was an IRA; she wanted to put the maximum of $2000 in each year. Because the earnings in an IRA accumulate tax-free, it is the best form of accumulating wealth for retirement, typically providing twice the rate of return that a comparable non-IRA account would provide in the long run. Laura wanted to invest an additional $2000 per year as well. Because she was very risk averse, she wanted only half her investments in stock; the other half was to be bonds. So, we advised her to make the bond investments in the IRA, and the stock, through a mutual fund. The tax reason is straightforward: if she sold stocks for a gain, the maximum tax rate for her was 20%. On the other hand, interest on the bonds, if owned outside the IRA, would be taxed at her higher 28% "normal" tax rate.

KIM

Kim's "sideline" business was going so well that she decided to devote more time to it, working just about every weekend. Curious? Hint: she drove a pink car. Worried about eventual retirement, we advised her to form a corporation for the business, and then set up a qualified corporate pension. She began socking away the maximum $30,000 per year, all tax deductible. This was far in excess of the $2000 per year she was saving through her IRA!

LESLIE AND BOB

This hard-working couple had built a successful optometry practice in a small town. They ran the business through a partnership, for legal liability purposes and tax purposes. The tax purpose was two-fold. First, partnerships don't pay taxes; so, they avoided the double tax that would have occurred if they formed a corporation. Second, their two daughters performed various tasks around the office—running errands, cleaning up, answering phones, etc. They were paid a salary, which was tax deductible by the partnership. Imagine being able to tax-deduct your kids' allowances!

GOOD TIME BARRY

Everyone recognized Barry. It was impossible to turn your tv on at night, and not see him pitching the furniture store with the jingle that everyone knows as well!

Barry has been the actor in these commercials for *years*. Everywhere he goes, people sing the jingle to him, and ask for his autograph. He's even been made fun of by many of the local radio personalities. He's a household name type of guy in his marketplace. By all measures, he would be considered a very successful and rich guy. In fact, many people think he is the owner of the furniture store or something. They don't realize he's an actor.

They also couldn't imagine that Barry is broke! Barry's attorney referred him to us. His lawyer wanted us to sit him down, and prepare a plan to follow for his money. (Or, we should say *lack of money!*)

See, Barry doesn't make much money. He only gets paid $2,000 for each commercial he does. (Which, as you might know, can number in the dozens each year!) Which mean's he will gross about $80,000 this year. Notice I said *gross*, not *net*!

Because Barry is so popular, and so well recognized, and everyone thinks he's rich, *he lives up to his image!* He spends money like water. H eats in the fancy restaurants, and goes to the most expensive shows. He portrays himself to be exactly what his image says he is. And he lives that way. The only problem is that he doesn't have enough money to live a Rolls Royce Lifestyle!

That's what led him in to see us. His attorney knew that at his age (63), he'd better start saving some cash for the future! When we met with Barry, the first thing we did was get a handle on his assets (hardly anything), and debts (which is a list as long as a yardstick!).

We recognized that his problem was not just financial. He admitted that he'd enjoyed living up to his image, and that he might need some counseling to deal with reality. He also agreed that he'd better start doing some things right away (especially when we showed him the graph of his retirement projection!).

He, in fact, went through some therapy to deal with his need for adulation, which really opened his eyes to how things really are! Once he started seeing the psychologist, he hired an agent to get him other bookings to make additional dough. Barry then decided to tone down his spending and make a commitment to retiring in a few years.

What a change! Barry began to do commercials for other companies in town, and took many similar jobs in other towns. He started doing personal appearances and other specialty gigs. He was amazed at how much better he felt when he was working, knowing that he was going to actually have something to show for it later on!

That was about a year ago. Now, Barry is finished with the psychologist. He has tripled his earnings. We would like to say he has doubled his savings, but since he had none to begin with, you can't multiply zeros! (He is now saving a big chunk of money each month into his qualified retirement plan.) His taxes have dropped by over 13% since implementing the tax strategies we recommended, and his girl friend is provided for if he were to pass away.

All in all, Barry is a happy camper. He had his time to play games, and fortunately, he didn't wait until it was too late! We're excited for him, and love seeing him on the tube at two in the morning, in the middle of an "I Dream of Jeannie" rerun! Keep your eyes out for him. If you're awake, I'm sure you'll see him too!

RACHEL'S DISAPPEARING RETIREMENT

"In times like these, it helps to remember that there have always been times like these!"

—Anonymous

Rachel had a hard time with the whole concept. She couldn't understand why what you see, isn't what you get.

It all started when she went to the doctor last week. (She goes to the chiropractor to help with her chronic backaches.) Anyway, while she was waiting for the doctor to see her, she started reading this article in one of the magazines sitting on the table in the waiting room. The title of the article caught her eye, because it was talking about a subject that is near and dear to her heart:

Miserably Low CD Rates!

Rachel is 72 years old, and had been retired for the last ten years. She remembers when she was getting 13% interest on her CD's when she first quit her job at the phone company, and took early retirement. She still remembers how she had more interest income, plus her retirement and Social Security income, than she needed to live. But that was then, and this is now! Over the last decade she has seen her interest rates plummet to below 3%. And there are no signs of things getting better.

See, for Rachel, just like millions of retirees in similar circumstances, low interest rates are bad. She's not trying to refinance a house (hers is paid off) She needs as much interest income as she can get.

Understand that Rachel isn't a spendthrift. She doesn't purchase things unless she really needs them. She doesn't overspend on extravagant clothing or fancy dinners. She lives a modest lifestyle. Anyway, when Rachel was reading this article, it finally made her realize why she was experience what she was experiencing:

Rachel was running out of money!

And she was plenty upset. Here's what she's been living through, and what the article said why it was happening to her. When she retired, she had over $80,000 in the bank, plus $1,190 per month of combined income. It seemed like plenty at the time. Now she had only $41,000 in the bank, with her retirement checks totaling only $1,387 a month.

At this rate, and with the way her expenses keep going up each month, she figures she'll be out of money in another six or seven years. Here's the real combination of problems: INFLATION AND TAXES ARE WIPING OUT HER MONEY! They team up to actually cause her to lose money, let alone make the lousy 3% she things she's making!

Let's see why "seeing isn't always believing." If she "sees" a 3% interest rate, then why isn't she making 3%? Here's why: Rachael is earning 3% interest on her CD's, and she is in the 28% tax bracket, which means her net, after taxes, yield only **2.16%!**

3.00% yield

x 28% tax = .84% lost to taxes

2.16% net after tax yield

Now, that would be bad enough, but we cannot forget about our friend, Inflation.

Yes, they *claim* inflation has been licked—that it is gone. Why? Because it's been hover around 3-4% for the last couple of years, and that is considered low, low by today's standards.

But, did you know that in the early '70's, when President Nixon instituted price controls, inflation was an *incredibly high 4%*! Isn't that interesting? That in 1972, 4$ inflation was considered so high, that the government tried putting price controls in place. Now, when inflation is at the same exact level 20 years later, it's considered insignificant by the boys in the Capital!

How can this be? Could it be that inflation has changed, or is it more likely that the government has changed the way they want us to view it? Anyway, how does this "not so bad" inflation affect our CD example? Well, remember that we're at 2.16% net, after tax yield. Now let's subtract inflation from this yield, to arrive at your true change in value, adjusted for the loss of purchasing power:

2.16% net, after tax yield

less   *3.50%* inflation

(1.34%) True return

Those brackets, by the way, mean a ***negative real rate of return!*** Yes, that means that Rachel has a loss of value, of $134 for each $10,000 she has invested in CD's!

So, what does Rachel do to get a better return, and avoid the new higher tax on their Social Security and other income? (See, Clinton's and Congress feel that Rachel is living too high off the hog, and needs to pay more taxes to balance the scales of society's justice. I mean, is this sick, or what? But don't get us started on the "geniuses" in Washington. By the way, these opinions apply across the board to all the politicians who are making Rachel's life more and more difficult. We don't care if they are Democrats, Republicans, Libertarians, or whatever. Hurting our nation's retirees with new taxes, in this low interest rate environment is just unconscionable.

As we said a couple of minutes ago, the real secret Rachel needs to know is how to invest in things that are off the "tax hit list"; and that will help her earn a rate of return that will keep up with her increases in living expenses. Oh sure, things like CD's and municipal bonds get special tax treatment.

So special, that *they cause the maximum taxes to be paid!* (The IRS has special plans for retirees who invest in CD's and muni bonds. It's called, GOTCHA!)

What we had Rachel do is figure out how much monthly income she needs, and then build a plan that used the tax favored items the government allows, to assure she gets the cash flow she needs, and avoid wasting money on the taxes she didn't need to be paying!

HAPPY CAMPERS

OK, this one has nothing to do with retirement, but we thought we'd offer up another "freebie" to you.

The IRS considers a day camp a form of child care. If you send your child to day camp, no matter what your income, you may qualify for the child and dependent care tax credit. The child must be under 13 and both parents must work, to qualify. The IRS allows as much as $480 for one child and $960 for two or more children. Generally the credit is equal to 20% of up to $2400 for one kid ($4800 for two or more children) of day care expenses. Just request a form 2441 form the IRS or your tax preparer, and attach it to your tax return!

If you want to see an example of tax-deductible contributions, there is an example in the Appendix at the end of the book

OK, you're now armed with 7 tax tricks to fight the tax man. Here's one more: if you buy this book to try to minimize your taxes, the book is tax deductible as a Miscellaneous itemized tax deduction on your Schedule A. Sweeeet....

Appendix

How to Use the Tax Styles

Chapter 2—Hobby Losses

Let's take a look at how Jimmy, our comic book and baseball card collecting friend, reports his hobby/business on his tax return.

First, we had him do an "inventory" of his collections, then come up with estimates of how much he paid for each book/card. Sometimes, he had to completely guess these amounts. Next, we had him figure the costs of the books and cards he sold in 1998: about $5000. Remember, he sold them for $30,000. Next, we had him add up his travel costs to a convention in Las Vegas, and one in New York. His airfare was $800, hotels $500, meals $250, and incidental (cab fare, etc) another $100.

Now, for his office expenses. Phone (all used for business) was $350. His office furniture yielded annual depreciation of $800. The office was about 1/10th of the square footage of the total house. So, since his house insurance was about $1200, he deducted 1/10th of that, or $120. We did the same thing with his annual gas and electric bills, providing $1500 in deductions. Finally, 1/10th of depreciation on the house itself gave another $900 per year in deductions.

So, how is this shown on a tax return? First, you have to file a "long form" 1040 (the short form 1040's won't do). Next, you have to attach a Schedule C to the 1040 to report the business. This form is easily obtainable from the IRS or a tax preparer. Finally, if you happen to make a profit for the year, like Jimmy, you need to attach a Schedule SE to your 1040. This is also easily obtained. This form is used to calculate possible extra Social Security and Medicare taxes.

A filled-out Schedule C, with related parts of his 1040, are shown for Jimmy on the following three pages. Because he deducts home office expenses, he also needs to attach a form 8829, which is also easily obtained.

Form **1040**	Department of the Treasury—Internal Revenue Service				
	U.S. Individual Income Tax Return	**1999**		IRS Use Only—Do not write or staple in this space.	

For the year Jan 1–Dec. 31, 1999, or other tax year beginning , 1999, ending . | OMB No. 1545-0074

Label
(See instructions on page 18.)
Use the IRS label. Otherwise, please print or type.

Your first name and initial	Last name	Your social security number
JIMMY		
If a joint return, spouse's first name and initial	Last name	Spouse's social security number

Home address (number and street). If you have a P.O. box, see page 18. | Apt. no.

City, town or post office, state, and ZIP code. If you have a foreign address, see page 18.

▲ **IMPORTANT!** ▲
You must enter your SSN(s) above.

Presidential Election Campaign (See page 18.)
Do you want $3 to go to this fund? . . . .
If a joint return, does your spouse want $3 to go to this fund? . . . . .

Yes | No | Note. Checking "Yes" will not change your tax or reduce your refund.

Filing Status
Check only one box.

1 ☐ Single
2 ☐ Married filing joint return (even if only one had income)
3 ☐ Married filing separate return. Enter spouse's social security no. above and full name here. ▶
4 ☐ Head of household (with qualifying person). (See page 18.) If the qualifying person is a child but not your dependent, enter this child's name here. ▶
5 ☐ Qualifying widow(er) with dependent child (year spouse died ▶ 19). (See page 18.)

Exemptions

6a ☐ Yourself. If your parent (or someone else) can claim you as a dependent on his or her tax return, do not check box 6a. . . . .
b ☐ Spouse . . . .
c Dependents:

(1) First name Last name	(2) Dependent's social security number	(3) Dependent's relationship to you	(4)✔ if qualifying child for child tax credit (see page 19)
			☐
			☐
			☐
			☐
			☐
			☐

If more than six dependents, see page 19.

No. of boxes checked on 6a and 6b _____
No. of your children on 6c who:
• lived with you _____
• did not live with you due to divorce or separation (see page 19) _____
Dependents on 6c not entered above _____
Add numbers entered on lines above ▶

d Total number of exemptions claimed . . . .

Income
Attach Copy B of your Forms W-2 and W-2G here. Also attach Form(s) 1099-R if tax was withheld.

If you did not get a W-2, see page 20.

Enclose, but do not staple, any payment. Also, please use Form 1040-V.

7	Wages, salaries, tips, etc. Attach Form(s) W-2	7
8a	Taxable interest. Attach Schedule B if required	8a
b	Tax-exempt interest. DO NOT include on line 8a . . . 8b	
9	Ordinary dividends. Attach Schedule B if required	9
10	Taxable refunds, credits, or offsets of state and local income taxes (see page 21) .	10
11	Alimony received	11
12	Business income or (loss). Attach Schedule C or C-EZ	12	21,330
13	Capital gain or (loss). Attach Schedule D if required. If not required, check here ▶ ☐	13
14	Other gains or (losses). Attach Form 4797	14
15a	Total IRA distributions . 15a	b Taxable amount (see page 22)	15b
16a	Total pensions and annuities 16a	b Taxable amount (see page 22)	16b
17	Rental real estate, royalties, partnerships, S corporations, trusts, etc. Attach Schedule E	17
18	Farm income or (loss). Attach Schedule F	18
19	Unemployment compensation	19
20a	Social security benefits . 20a	b Taxable amount (see page 24)	20b
21	Other income. List type and amount (see page 24)	21
22	Add the amounts in the far right column for lines 7 through 21. This is your **total income** ▶	22

Adjusted Gross Income

23	IRA deduction (see page 26) 23	
24	Student loan interest deduction (see page 26) 24	
25	Medical savings account deduction. Attach Form 8853 . 25	
26	Moving expenses. Attach Form 3903 . . . 26	
27	One-half of self-employment tax. Attach Schedule SE . 27	
28	Self-employed health insurance deduction (see page 28) . 28	
29	Keogh and self-employed SEP and SIMPLE plans . . 29	
30	Penalty on early withdrawal of savings 30	
31a	Alimony paid b Recipient's SSN ▶ 31a	
32	Add lines 23 through 31a	32
33	Subtract line 32 from line 22. This is your **adjusted gross income** . . . ▶	33

For Disclosure, Privacy Act, and Paperwork Reduction Act Notice, see page 54. | Cat. No. 11320B | Form **1040** (1999)

SCHEDULE C (Form 1040)	**Profit or Loss From Business**	OMB No. 1545-0074
	(Sole Proprietorship)	**1999**
Department of the Treasury Internal Revenue Service (99)	▶ Partnerships, joint ventures, etc., must file Form 1065 or Form 1065-B. ▶ Attach to Form 1040 or Form 1041. ▶ See Instructions for Schedule C (Form 1040).	Attachment Sequence No. 09

Name of proprietor	Social security number (SSN)
JIMMY	

A. Principal business or profession, including product or service (see page C-1)
   B. Enter code from pages C-8 & 9 ▶

C. Business name. If no separate business name, leave blank.
   D. Employer ID number (EIN), if any

E. Business address (including suite or room no.) ▶
   City, town or post office, state, and ZIP code

F. Accounting method: (1) ☐ Cash (2) ☐ Accrual (3) ☐ Other (specify) ▶

G. Did you "materially participate" in the operation of this business during 1999? If "No," see page C-2 for limit on losses. ☐ Yes ☐ No

H. If you started or acquired this business during 1999, check here ▶ ☐

Part I — Income

1	Gross receipts or sales. **Caution:** If this income was reported to you on Form W-2 and the "Statutory employee" box on that form was checked, see page C-2 and check here ▶ ☐	1	30,000
2	Returns and allowances	2	
3	Subtract line 2 from line 1	3	30,000
4	Cost of goods sold (from line 42 on page 2)	4	5,000
5	**Gross profit.** Subtract line 4 from line 3	5	25,000
6	Other income, including Federal and state gasoline or fuel tax credit or refund (see page C-3)	6	
7	**Gross income.** Add lines 5 and 6 ▶	7	25,000

Part II — Expenses. Enter expenses for business use of your home **only** on line 30.

8	Advertising	8		19	Pension and profit-sharing plans	19	
9	Bad debts from sales or services (see page C-3)	9		20	Rent or lease (see page C-4):		
10	Car and truck expenses (see page C-3)	10		a	Vehicles, machinery, and equipment	20a	
11	Commissions and fees	11		b	Other business property	20b	
12	Depletion	12		21	Repairs and maintenance	21	
13	Depreciation and section 179 expense deduction (not included in Part III) (see page C-3)	13		22	Supplies (not included in Part III)	22	
				23	Taxes and licenses	23	
14	Employee benefit programs (other than on line 19)	14		24	Travel, meals, and entertainment:		
15	Insurance (other than health)	15		a	Travel	24a	
16	Interest:			b	Meals and entertainment		
a	Mortgage (paid to banks, etc.)	16a		c	Enter nondeductible amount included on line 24b (see page C-5)		
b	Other	16b		d	Subtract line 24c from line 24b	24d	
17	Legal and professional services	17		25	Utilities	25	
18	Office expense	18		26	Wages (less employment credits)	26	
				27	Other expenses (from line 48 on page 2)	27	

28	Total expenses before expenses for business use of home. Add lines 8 through 27 in columns ▶	28	
29	Tentative profit (loss). Subtract line 28 from line 7	29	
30	Expenses for business use of your home. Attach **Form 8829**	30	3,670
31	**Net profit or (loss).** Subtract line 30 from line 29. • If a profit, enter on **Form 1040, line 12,** and ALSO on **Schedule SE, line 2** (statutory employees, see page C-6). Estates and trusts, enter on Form 1041, line 3. • If a loss, you MUST go on to line 32.	31	21,330

32 If you have a loss, check the box that describes your investment in this activity (see page C-6).
   • If you checked 32a, enter the loss on **Form 1040, line 12,** and ALSO on **Schedule SE, line 2** (statutory employees, see page C-6). Estates and trusts, enter on Form 1041, line 3.
   • If you checked 32b, you MUST attach **Form 6198.**
   32a ☐ All investment is at risk.
   32b ☐ Some investment is not at risk.

For Paperwork Reduction Act Notice, see Form 1040 instructions.   Cat. No. 11334P   Schedule C (Form 1040) 1999

Chapter 3—Charitable Contributions

Reporting a charitable contribution on your taxes is not that difficult. First, you have to file a long form 1040. Then, attach a Schedule A, which shows charitable contributions. The Schedule A is easily obtained from the IRS or a tax practitioner. In addition, if you donate any non-cash items, and the total deduction for them is more than $500 for the year, then you must also attach a Form 8283, which gives more information on non-cash contributions. This form is easily obtained from the IRS or a tax practitioner.

To see this in action, let's take the example of Billy's old clunker car. Let's say he bought it in 1965 (new) for $2800. He the blue book value on it now is $800. With a simple phone to call to his local charity, they come and tow it away, giving him a receipt. To add more documentation, he takes a last photo of his beloved car, and puts in his tax files. He takes a tax deduction for $800, as shown on the following tax forms. Note that you only need an appraisal for a property gift if it exceeds $5000, so he's off the hook for an appraisal.

The next few pages show how Billy deducts his contribution.

SCHEDULES A&B (Form 1040) Department of the Treasury Internal Revenue Service (90)	**Schedule A—Itemized Deductions** (Schedule B is on back) ▶ Attach to Form 1040. ▶ See Instructions for Schedules A and B (Form 1040).			OMB No. 1545-0074 19**99** Attachment Sequence No. 07
Name(s) shown on Form 1040 **BILLY**				Your social security number

Medical and Dental Expenses		Caution. Do not include expenses reimbursed or paid by others.				
	1	Medical and dental expenses (see page A-1)	1			
	2	Enter amount from Form 1040, line 34 . | 2 |				
	3	Multiply line 2 above by 7.5% (.075)	3			
	4	Subtract line 3 from line 1. If line 3 is more than line 1, enter -0-			4	
Taxes You Paid (See page A-2.)	5	State and local income taxes	5			
	6	Real estate taxes (see page A-2)	6			
	7	Personal property taxes	7			
	8	Other taxes. List type and amount ▶	8			
	9	Add lines 5 through 8			9	
Interest You Paid (See page A-3.) Note. Personal interest is not deductible.	10	Home mortgage interest and points reported to you on Form 1098	10			
	11	Home mortgage interest not reported to you on Form 1098. If paid to the person from whom you bought the home, see page A-3 and show that person's name, identifying no., and address ▶	11			
	12	Points not reported to you on Form 1098. See page A-3 for special rules . . .	12			
	13	Investment interest. Attach Form 4952 if required. (See page A-3.)	13			
	14	Add lines 10 through 13			14	
Gifts to Charity If you made a gift and got a benefit for it, see page A-4.	15	Gifts by cash or check. If you made any gift of $250 or more, see page A-4	15			
	16	Other than by cash or check. If any gift of $250 or more, see page A-4. You **MUST** attach Form 8283 if over $500	16	800		
	17	Carryover from prior year	17			
	18	Add lines 15 through 17			18	
Casualty and Theft Losses	19	Casualty or theft loss(es). Attach Form 4684. (See page A-5.)			19	
Job Expenses and Most Other Miscellaneous Deductions (See page A-6 for expenses to deduct here.)	20	Unreimbursed employee expenses—job travel, union dues, job education, etc. You **MUST** attach Form 2106 or 2106-EZ if required. (See page A-5.) ▶	20			
	21	Tax preparation fees	21			
	22	Other expenses—investment, safe deposit box, etc. List type and amount ▶...........................	22			
	23	Add lines 20 through 22	23			
	24	Enter amount from Form 1040, line 34 . | 24 |				
	25	Multiply line 24 above by 2% (.02) . . .	25			
	26	Subtract line 25 from line 23. If line 25 is more than line 23, enter -0-			26	
Other Miscellaneous Deductions	27	Other—from list on page A-6. List type and amount ▶			27	
Total Itemized Deductions	28	Is Form 1040, line 34, over $126,600 (over $63,300 if married filing separately)? ☐ **No.** Your deduction is not limited. Add the amounts in the far right column for lines 4 through 27. Also, enter this amount on Form 1040, line 36. ☐ **Yes.** Your deduction may be limited. See page A-6 for the amount to enter.	} ▶		28	

For Paperwork Reduction Act Notice, see Form 1040 Instructions.   Cat. No. 11330X   Schedule A (Form 1040) 1999

Form **8283**	**Noncash Charitable Contributions**	OMB No. 1545-0908
(Rev. October 1998)	▶ Attach to your tax return if you claimed a total deduction of over $500 for all contributed property.	Attachment Sequence No. **55**
Department of the Treasury Internal Revenue Service	▶ See separate instructions.	

Name(s) shown on your income tax return | Identifying number

BILLY

Note: *Figure the amount of your contribution deduction before completing this form. See your tax return instructions.*

Section A—List in this section **only** items (or groups of similar items) for which you claimed a deduction of $5,000 or less. Also, list certain publicly traded securities even if the deduction is over $5,000 (see instructions).

Part I Information on Donated Property—If you need more space, attach a statement.

1	(a) Name and address of the donee organization	(b) Description of donated property
A	"LOCAL CHARITY"	USED CAR
B		
C		
D		
E		

Note: *If the amount you claimed as a deduction for an item is $500 or less, you do not have to complete columns (d), (e), and (f).*

	(c) Date of the contribution	(d) Date acquired by donor (mo., yr.)	(e) How acquired by donor	(f) Donor's cost or adjusted basis	(g) Fair market value	(h) Method used to determine the fair market value
A	1998	1965	PURCHASE	2,800	800	BLUE BOOK
B						
C						
D						
E						

Part II Other Information—Complete line 2 if you gave less than an entire interest in property listed in Part I. Complete line 3 if conditions were attached to a contribution listed in Part I.

2 If, during the year, you contributed less than the entire interest in the property, complete lines a–e.

  a Enter the letter from Part I that identifies the property ▶ _____ . If Part II applies to more than one property, attach a separate statement.

  b Total amount claimed as a deduction for the property listed in Part I: **(1)** For this tax year ▶ _____

                                      (2) For any prior tax years ▶ _____

  c Name and address of each organization to which any such contribution was made in a prior year (complete only if different from the donee organization above):

    Name of charitable organization (donee)

    Address (number, street, and room or suite no.)

    City or town, state, and ZIP code

  d For tangible property, enter the place where the property is located or kept ▶ _____

  e Name of any person, other than the donee organization, having actual possession of the property ▶ _____

3 If conditions were attached to any contribution listed in Part I, answer questions a – c and attach the required statement (see instructions).

		Yes	No
a	Is there a restriction, either temporary or permanent, on the donee's right to use or dispose of the donated property?		
b	Did you give to anyone (other than the donee organization or another organization participating with the donee organization in cooperative fundraising) the right to the income from the donated property or to the possession of the property, including the right to vote donated securities, to acquire the property by purchase or otherwise, or to designate the person having such income, possession, or right to acquire?		
c	Is there a restriction limiting the donated property for a particular use?		

For Paperwork Reduction Act Notice, see page 4 of separate instructions.   Cat. No. 62299J   Form **8283** (Rev. 10-98)

Chapter 4—Real Estate

Here's an example of how to report a rental property on your taxes. We'll discuss Pamela, who bought the vacation condo on the beach. To avoid hassles she used a property management company to find renters, for which she paid a 15% commission.

He's the info on her condo for 1999:

Rental income		$10,000
Expenses:		
Prop. Management fees		1,500
Utilities		500
Condo Assoc. fees		1,000
Repairs, maintenance, clng.		1,000
Insurance		500
Mortgage interest	5,000	3,500
Profit before depreciation		500
Less: depreciation (on condo and furniture)		<3,500>
Tax loss		<3,000>

At her 28% bracket, the rental property provides almost $900 per year in tax savings.

Notice that the tax loss isn't a real loss—it's all driven by the "paper loss" of depreciation.[16] So, the actual cash flow from the property is $500 (from operations) plus about $900 from tax savings. And the best part, the renters are paying down her mortgage.

---

16 A warning here. When Pamela eventually sells the condo, she'll pay more taxes on the gain due to depreciation taken.

To report income from a rental property, you need to attach a Schedule E (easily obtained from the IRS or a tax preparer) to your 1040. A filled-in Schedule E, and 1040, is shown for Pamela in the next few pages.

Form **1040**	Department of the Treasury—Internal Revenue Service **U.S. Individual Income Tax Return** **19**99		IRS Use Only—Do no

For the year Jan. 1–Dec. 31, 1999, or other tax year beginning _____ , 1999, ending _____

Label
(See instructions on page 18.)

Use the IRS label. Otherwise, please print or type.

L A B E L · H E R E

Your first name and initial	Last name
PAMELA	
If a joint return, spouse's first name and initial	Last name

Home address (number and street). If you have a P.O. box, see page 18.	Apt. no.

City, town or post office, state, and ZIP code. If you have a foreign address, see page 18.

Presidential Election Campaign (See page 18.) ▶

Do you want $3 to go to this fund? . . . .
If a joint return, does your spouse want $3 to go to this fund? . . . .

Filing Status

Check only one box.

1 ☐ Single
2 ☐ Married filing joint return (even if only one had income)
3 ☐ Married filing separate return. Enter spouse's social security no. above and full name here. ▶
4 ☐ Head of household (with qualifying person). (See page 18.) If the qualifying person is enter this child's name here. ▶
5 ☐ Qualifying widow(er) with dependent child (year spouse died ▶ 19). (See

Exemptions

If more than six dependents, see page 19.

6a ☐ **Yourself.** If your parent (or someone else) can claim you as a dependent on his or he return, **do not** check box 6a . . . .
b ☐ **Spouse** . . . .

c Dependents:		(2) Dependent's social security number	(3) Dependent's relationship to you	(4)✓ If qua child for chi credit (see pa
(1) First name	Last name			
				☐
				☐
				☐
				☐

d Total number of exemptions claimed . . . .

Income

Attach Copy B of your Forms W-2 and W-2G here. Also attach Form(s) 1099-R if tax was withheld.

If you did not get a W-2, see page 20.

Enclose, but do not staple, any payment. Also, please use Form 1040-V.

7 Wages, salaries, tips, etc. Attach Form(s) W-2 . . . . . .
8a **Taxable** interest. Attach Schedule B if required . . . . .
b Tax-exempt interest. DO NOT include on line 8a . . . | 8b |
9 Ordinary dividends. Attach Schedule B if required . . . .
10 Taxable refunds, credits, or offsets of state and local income taxes (see page 21) . . .
11 Alimony received . . . .
12 Business income or (loss). Attach Schedule C or C-EZ . . . .
13 Capital gain or (loss). Attach Schedule D if required. If not required, check here ▶ ☐
14 Other gains or (losses). Attach Form 4797 . . . .
15a Total IRA distributions . | 15a | b Taxable amount (see page 22)
16a Total pensions and annuities | 16a | b Taxable amount (see page 22)
17 Rental real estate, royalties, partnerships, S corporations, trusts, etc. Attach Schedule E
18 Farm income or (loss). Attach Schedule F . . . .
19 Unemployment compensation . . . .
20a Social security benefits . | 20a | b Taxable amount (see page 24)
21 Other income. List type and amount (see page 24) . . . .
22 Add the amounts in the far right column for lines 7 through 21. This is your **total income** ▶

Adjusted Gross

23 IRA deduction (see page 26) . . . . | 23 |
24 Student loan interest deduction (see page 26) . . . . | 24 |
25 Medical savings account deduction. Attach Form 8853 . | 25 |

SCHEDULE E	**Supplemental Income and Loss**	OMB No. 1545-0074
(Form 1040)	(From rental real estate, royalties, partnerships, S corporations, estates, trusts, REMICs, etc.)	19**99**
Department of the Treasury Internal Revenue Service (99)	▶ Attach to Form 1040 or Form 1041. ▶ See Instructions for Schedule E (Form 1040).	Attachment Sequence No. 13

Name(s) shown on return	Your social security number
PAMELA	

Part I Income or Loss From Rental Real Estate and Royalties Note: *Report income and expenses from your business of renting personal property on **Schedule C** or **C-EZ** (see page E-1). Report farm rental income or loss from **Form 4835** on page 2, line 39.*

				Yes	No
1	Show the kind and location of each **rental real estate property**:	2 For each rental real estate property listed on line 1, did you or your family use it during the tax year for personal purposes for more than the greater of:			
A	....		A		
B	....	• 14 days, **or**	B		✔
C	....	• 10% of the total days rented at fair rental value? (See page E-1.)	C		✔

			Properties			Totals
			A	B	C	(Add columns A, B, and C.)
Income:						
3	Rents received	3				3
4	Royalties received	4				4
Expenses:						
5	Advertising	5				
6	Auto and travel (see page E-2) .	6				
7	Cleaning and maintenance . . .	7				
8	Commissions	8				
9	Insurance	9				
10	Legal and other professional fees	10				
11	Management fees	11				
12	Mortgage interest paid to banks, etc. (see page E-2)	12				12
13	Other interest	13				
14	Repairs	14				
15	Supplies	15				
16	Taxes	16				
17	Utilities	17				
18	Other (list) ▶	18				
19	Add lines 5 through 18	19				19
20	Depreciation expense or depletion (see page E-3)	20				20
21	Total expenses. Add lines 19 and 20	21				
22	Income or (loss) from rental real estate or royalty properties. Subtract line 21 from line 3 (rents) or line 4 (royalties). If the result is a (loss), see page E-3 to find out if you must file **Form 6198** . .	22				
23	Deductible rental real estate loss. **Caution:** *Your rental real estate loss on line 22 may be limited. See page E-3 to find out if you must file **Form 8582**. Real estate professionals must complete line 42 on page 2*	23	(	)(	)(	)	
24	**Income.** Add positive amounts shown on line 22. **Do not** include any losses				24	
25	**Losses.** Add royalty losses from line 22 and rental real estate losses from line 23. Enter total losses here				25	(| 500 |)
26	**Total** rental real estate and royalty income or (loss). Combine lines 24 and 25. Enter the result here. If Parts II, III, IV, and line 39 on page 2 do not apply to you, also enter this amount on Form 1040, line 17. Otherwise, include this amount in the total on line 40 on page 2				26	(500)

For Paperwork Reduction Act Notice, see Form 1040 instructions.   Cat. No. 11344L   Schedule E (Form 1040) 1999

Chapter 5—Trusts

To see how taxes work for a trust, let's look back at Bobby, our country-western star. Recall that he put his real estate investments into a trust. Because he had control over it, the earnings were all taxed to him.[17]

When we added up all his earnings, the net was about $1.2 million. We show how to report trust earnings by attaching a Schedule E (easily obtained from the IRS or a tax practitioner) to your long-form 1040, as shown in the next couple of pages. One word of caution: the trust's income must first be reported on a Form 1041, which is filed with IRS. Kids, don't try this one at home—get a tax practitioner to fill out this complicated form for you.

---

17 This, like most grantor/single owner trusts, is called a "simple trust" in the tax code, which means that the income is taxed to the grantor. There also exist "complex trusts", which are often set up for children or grandchildren, and will not distribute income to them until they reach a certain age. The earnings not distributed to the beneficiaries, in a complex trust, are taxed to the trust itself.

Form **1040**	Department of the Treasury—Internal Revenue Service **U.S. Individual Income Tax Return** **1999**		IRS Use Only—Do not write or staple in this space.

For the year Jan. 1–Dec. 31, 1999, or other tax year beginning , 1999, ending . | OMB No. 1545-0074

Label
(See instructions on page 18.)
Use the IRS label. Otherwise, please print or type.

Your first name and initial: **BOBBY**   Last name

If a joint return, spouse's first name and initial   Last name

Home address (number and street). If you have a P.O. box, see page 18.   Apt. no.

City, town or post office, state, and ZIP code. If you have a foreign address, see page 18.

Your social security number

Spouse's social security number

▲ **IMPORTANT!** ▲
You must enter your SSN(s) above.

Presidential Election Campaign (See page 18.)
Do you want $3 to go to this fund? . . . .
If a joint return, does your spouse want $3 to go to this fund? .

Yes | No | Note. Checking "Yes" will not change your tax or reduce your refund.

Filing Status
Check only one box.

1 ☐ Single
2 ☐ Married filing joint return (even if only one had income)
3 ☐ Married filing separate return. Enter spouse's social security no. above and full name here. ▶
4 ☐ Head of household (with qualifying person). (See page 18.) If the qualifying person is a child but not your dependent, enter this child's name here. ▶
5 ☐ Qualifying widow(er) with dependent child (year spouse died ▶ 19). (See page 18.)

Exemptions

6a ☐ Yourself. If your parent (or someone else) can claim you as a dependent on his or her tax return, do not check box 6a. . . . .
b ☐ Spouse . . . .
c Dependents:

(1) First name Last name	(2) Dependent's social security number	(3) Dependent's relationship to you	(4)✔ If qualifying child for child tax credit (see page 19)
			☐
			☐
			☐
			☐
			☐
			☐

If more than six dependents, see page 19.

No. of boxes checked on 6a and 6b
No. of your children on 6c who:
• lived with you
• did not live with you due to divorce or separation (see page 19)
Dependents on 6c not entered above
Add numbers entered on lines above ▶

d Total number of exemptions claimed . . . .

Income

Attach Copy B of your Forms W-2 and W-2G here. Also attach Form(s) 1099-R if tax was withheld.

If you did not get a W-2, see page 20.

Enclose, but do not staple, any payment. Also, please use Form 1040-V.

7	Wages, salaries, tips, etc. Attach Form(s) W-2	7	
8a	Taxable interest. Attach Schedule B if required	8a	
b	Tax-exempt interest. DO NOT include on line 8a . . .	8b	
9	Ordinary dividends. Attach Schedule B if required . . .	9	
10	Taxable refunds, credits, or offsets of state and local income taxes (see page 21) .	10	
11	Alimony received	11	
12	Business income or (loss). Attach Schedule C or C-EZ . .	12	
13	Capital gain or (loss). Attach Schedule D if required. If not required, check here ▶ ☐	13	
14	Other gains or (losses). Attach Form 4797	14	
15a	Total IRA distributions . 15a	b Taxable amount (see page 22)	15b	
16a	Total pensions and annuities 16a	b Taxable amount (see page 22)	16b	
17	Rental real estate, royalties, partnerships, S corporations, trusts, etc. Attach Schedule E	17	1,200,000
18	Farm income or (loss). Attach Schedule F	18	
19	Unemployment compensation	19	
20a	Social security benefits . 20a	b Taxable amount (see page 24)	20b	
21	Other income. List type and amount (see page 24) . . .	21	
22	Add the amounts in the far right column for lines 7 through 21. This is your total income ▶	22	

Adjusted Gross Income

23	IRA deduction (see page 26)	23	
24	Student loan interest deduction (see page 26) . .	24	
25	Medical savings account deduction. Attach Form 8853 .	25	
26	Moving expenses. Attach Form 3903	26	
27	One-half of self-employment tax. Attach Schedule SE .	27	
28	Self-employed health insurance deduction (see page 28)	28	
29	Keogh and self-employed SEP and SIMPLE plans . .	29	
30	Penalty on early withdrawal of savings	30	
31a	Alimony paid b Recipient's SSN ▶	31a	
32	Add lines 23 through 31a	32	
33	Subtract line 32 from line 22. This is your adjusted gross income . . . ▶	33	

For Disclosure, Privacy Act, and Paperwork Reduction Act Notice, see page 54.   Cat. No. 11320B   Form **1040** (1999)

SCHEDULE E (Form 1040) Department of the Treasury Internal Revenue Service (99)	**Supplemental Income and Loss** (From rental real estate, royalties, partnerships, S corporations, estates, trusts, REMICs, etc.) ▶ Attach to Form 1040 or Form 1041. ▶ See Instructions for Schedule E (Form 1040).	OMB No. 1545-0074 19**99** Attachment Sequence No. **13**

Name(s) shown on return
BOBBY   Your social security number

Part I Income or Loss From Rental Real Estate and Royalties Note: *Report income and expenses from your business of renting personal property on **Schedule C** or **C-EZ** (see page E-1). Report farm rental income or loss from **Form 4835** on page 2, line 39.*

1 Show the kind and location of each **rental real estate property**:	2 For each rental real estate property listed on line 1, did you or your family use it during the tax year for personal purposes for more than the greater of:	Yes	No
A	• 14 days, or	A	
B	• 10% of the total days rented at fair rental value?	B	
C	(See page E-1.)	C	

Income:		Properties			Totals (Add columns A, B, and C.)
		A	B	C	
3 Rents received	**3**				**3**
4 Royalties received	**4**				**4**
Expenses:					
5 Advertising	**5**				
6 Auto and travel (see page E-2) .	**6**				
7 Cleaning and maintenance . .	**7**				
8 Commissions	**8**				
9 Insurance	**9**				
10 Legal and other professional fees	**10**				
11 Management fees	**11**				
12 Mortgage interest paid to banks, etc. (see page E-2)	**12**				**12**
13 Other interest	**13**				
14 Repairs	**14**				
15 Supplies	**15**				
16 Taxes	**16**				
17 Utilities	**17**				
18 Other (list) ▶	**18**				
19 Add lines 5 through 18	**19**				**19**
20 Depreciation expense or depletion (see page E-3)	**20**				**20**
21 Total expenses. Add lines 19 and 20	**21**				
22 Income or (loss) from rental real estate or royalty properties. Subtract line 21 from line 3 (rents) or line 4 (royalties). If the result is a (loss), see page E-3 to find out if you must file **Form 6198**. . .	**22**				
23 Deductible rental real estate loss. **Caution:** *Your rental real estate loss on line 22 may be limited. See page E-3 to find out if you must file **Form 6582.** Real estate professionals must complete line 42 on page 2*	**23**	(	)(	)(	)
24 **Income.** Add positive amounts shown on line 22. **Do not** include any losses				**24**	
25 **Losses.** Add royalty losses from line 22 and rental real estate losses from line 23. Enter total losses here				**25**	( )
26 Total rental real estate and royalty income or (loss). Combine lines 24 and 25. Enter the result here. If Parts II, III, IV, and line 39 on page 2 do not apply to you, also enter this amount on Form 1040, line 17. Otherwise, include this amount in the total on line 40 on page 2				**26**	

For Paperwork Reduction Act Notice, see Form 1040 instructions.   Cat. No. 11344L   Schedule E (Form 1040) 1999

Schedule E (Form 1040) 1999		Attachment Sequence No. **13**		Page **2**

Name(s) shown on return. Do not enter name and social security number if shown on other side.

BOBBY

Your social security number

Note: *If you report amounts from farming or fishing on Schedule E, you must enter your gross income from those activities on line 41 below. Real estate professionals must complete line 42 below.*

Part II   Income or Loss From Partnerships and S Corporations Note: *If you report a loss from an at-risk activity, you MUST check either column (e) or (f) on line 27 to describe your investment in the activity. See page E-5. If you check column (f), you must attach Form 6198.*

27	(a) Name	(b) Enter P for partnership; S for S corporation	(c) Check if foreign partnership	(d) Employer identification number	Investment At Risk? (e) All is (f) Some is at risk / not at risk
A					
B					
C					
D					
E					

	Passive Income and Loss		Nonpassive Income and Loss		
	(g) Passive loss allowed (attach Form 8582 if required)	(h) Passive income from Schedule K-1	(i) Nonpassive loss from Schedule K-1	(j) Section 179 expense deduction from Form 4562	(k) Nonpassive income from Schedule K-1
A					
B					
C					
D					
E					

28a	Totals					
b	Totals					

29	Add columns (h) and (k) of line 28a	29	
30	Add columns (g), (i), and (j) of line 28b	30 (	)
31	Total partnership and S corporation income or (loss). Combine lines 29 and 30. Enter the result here and include in the total on line 40 below	31	

Part III   Income or Loss From Estates and Trusts

32	(a) Name	(b) Employer identification number
A		
B		

	Passive Income and Loss		Nonpassive Income and Loss		
	(c) Passive deduction or loss allowed (attach Form 8582 if required)	(d) Passive income from Schedule K-1	(e) Deduction or loss from Schedule K-1	(f) Other income from Schedule K-1	
A		1,200,000			
B					

33a	Totals				
b	Totals				

34	Add columns (d) and (f) of line 33a	34	1,200,000
35	Add columns (c) and (e) of line 33b	35 (	)
36	Total estate and trust income or (loss). Combine lines 34 and 35. Enter the result here and include in the total on line 40 below	36	1,200,000

Part IV   Income or Loss From Real Estate Mortgage Investment Conduits (REMICs)—Residual Holder

37	(a) Name	(b) Employer identification number	(c) Excess inclusion from Schedules Q, line 2c (see page E-6)	(d) Taxable income (net loss) from Schedules Q, line 1b	(e) Income from Schedules Q, line 3b

38	Combine columns (d) and (e) only. Enter the result here and include in the total on line 40 below	38	

Part V   Summary

39	Net farm rental income or (loss) from Form 4835. Also, complete line 41 below	39	
40	TOTAL income or (loss). Combine lines 26, 31, 36, 38, and 39. Enter the result here and on Form 1040, line 17 ▶	40	1,200,000

41	Reconciliation of Farming and Fishing Income. Enter your gross farming and fishing income reported on Form 4835, line 7; Schedule K-1 (Form 1065), line 15b; Schedule K-1 (Form 1120S), line 23; and Schedule K-1 (Form 1041), line 14 (see page E-6)	41	
42	Reconciliation for Real Estate Professionals. If you were a real estate professional (see page E-4), enter the net income or (loss) you reported anywhere on Form 1040 from all rental real estate activities in which you materially participated under the passive activity loss rules . . .	42	

Schedule E (Form 1040) 1999

Chapter 6—Tax Tricks for Stock Trading

We thought about showing you how to report stock gains and losses on you tax return. It's just that…it's kinda complicated. You should get a tax practitioner to do it for you. Such gains and losses are reported on a Schedule D (easily obtained from the IRS or a tax practitioner), which attaches to your long-form 1040.

Instead, we thought we'd show you how to deduct a non-business bad debt. Remember Susan, whose deadbeat boyfriend borrowed $4000, and walked? OK, she reports this on a Schedule D, which we show in the next few pages. Remember, because the tax code allows a maximum of 3k per year for net capital losses, she has to wait until next year to deduct the extra $1000.

Form **1040** Department of the Treasury—Internal Revenue Service
U.S. Individual Income Tax Return 19**99** IRS Use Only—Do not write or staple in this space.

For the year Jan. 1–Dec. 31, 1999, or other tax year beginning _____ , 1999, ending _____ OMB No. 1545-0074

Label
(See instructions on page 18.)

Use the IRS label. Otherwise, please print or type.

Your first name and initial SUSAN	Last name
If a joint return, spouse's first name and initial	Last name
Home address (number and street). If you have a P.O. box, see page 18.	Apt. no.
City, town or post office, state, and ZIP code. If you have a foreign address, see page 18.	

Your social security number

Spouse's social security number

▲ **IMPORTANT!** ▲
You **must** enter your SSN(s) above.

Presidential Election Campaign (See page 18.)

Do you want $3 to go to this fund? . . . .
If a joint return, does your spouse want $3 to go to this fund? . . . .

Yes | No | Note. Checking "Yes" will not change your tax or reduce your refund.

Filing Status

Check only one box.

1 ☐ Single
2 ☐ Married filing joint return (even if only one had income)
3 ☐ Married filing separate return. Enter spouse's social security no. above and full name here. ►
4 ☐ Head of household (with qualifying person). (See page 18.) If the qualifying person is a child but not your dependent, enter this child's name here. ►
5 ☐ Qualifying widow(er) with dependent child (year spouse died ► 19___). (See page 18.)

Exemptions

If more than six dependents, see page 19.

6a ☐ Yourself. If your parent (or someone else) can claim you as a dependent on his or her tax return, **do not** check box 6a.
b ☐ Spouse . . . .

c Dependents:

(1) First name Last name	(2) Dependent's social security number	(3) Dependent's relationship to you	(4) ✓ if qualifying child for child tax credit (see page 19)
			☐
			☐
			☐
			☐
			☐
			☐

No. of boxes checked on 6a and 6b

No. of your children on 6c who:
• lived with you
• did not live with you due to divorce or separation (see page 19)

Dependents on 6c not entered above

Add numbers entered on lines above ►

d Total number of exemptions claimed . . . .

Income

Attach Copy B of your Forms W-2 and W-2G here. Also attach Form(s) 1099-R if tax was withheld.

If you did not get a W-2, see page 20.

Enclose, but do not staple, any payment. Also, please use Form 1040-V.

7 Wages, salaries, tips, etc. Attach Form(s) W-2 . . . . | 7 | |
8a Taxable interest. Attach Schedule B if required . . . . . . | 8a | |
b Tax-exempt interest. DO NOT include on line 8a . . | 8b | |
9 Ordinary dividends. Attach Schedule B if required . . . . . . | 9 | |
10 Taxable refunds, credits, or offsets of state and local income taxes (see page 21) . . | 10 | |
11 Alimony received . . . . | 11 | |
12 Business income or (loss). Attach Schedule C or C-EZ . . . . | 12 | |
13 Capital gain or (loss). Attach Schedule D if required. If not required, check here ► ☐ | 13 | (3,000) |
14 Other gains or (losses). Attach Form 4797 . . . . | 14 | |
15a Total IRA distributions . | 15a | | b Taxable amount (see page 22) | 15b | |
16a Total pensions and annuities | 16a | | b Taxable amount (see page 22) | 16b | |
17 Rental real estate, royalties, partnerships, S corporations, trusts, etc. Attach Schedule E | 17 | |
18 Farm income or (loss). Attach Schedule F . . . . | 18 | |
19 Unemployment compensation . . . . | 19 | |
20a Social security benefits | 20a | | b Taxable amount (see page 24) | 20b | |
21 Other income. List type and amount (see page 24) _____ | 21 | |
22 Add the amounts in the far right column for lines 7 through 21. This is your **total income** ► | 22 | |

Adjusted Gross Income

23 IRA deduction (see page 25) . . . . | 23 | |
24 Student loan interest deduction (see page 26) . . . . | 24 | |
25 Medical savings account deduction. Attach Form 8853 . . | 25 | |
26 Moving expenses. Attach Form 3903 . . . . | 26 | |
27 One-half of self-employment tax. Attach Schedule SE . | 27 | |
28 Self-employed health insurance deduction (see page 28) . | 28 | |
29 Keogh and self-employed SEP and SIMPLE plans . . | 29 | |
30 Penalty on early withdrawal of savings . . . . | 30 | |
31a Alimony paid b Recipient's SSN ► _____ | 31a | |
32 Add lines 23 through 31a . . . . | 32 | |
33 Subtract line 32 from line 22. This is your **adjusted gross income** ► | 33 | |

For Disclosure, Privacy Act, and Paperwork Reduction Act Notice, see page 54. Cat. No. 11320B Form **1040** (1999)

SCHEDULE D
(Form 1040)

Department of the Treasury
Internal Revenue Service   (99)

Capital Gains and Losses

▶ Attach to Form 1040.   ▶ See Instructions for Schedule D (Form 1040).

▶ Use Schedule D-1 for more space to list transactions for lines 1 and 8.

OMB No. 1545-0074

1999

Attachment
Sequence No. **12**

Name(s) shown on Form 1040
SUSAN

Your social security number

Part I   Short-Term Capital Gains and Losses—Assets Held One Year or Less

(a) Description of property (Example: 100 sh. XYZ Co.)	(b) Date acquired (Mo., day, yr.)	(c) Date sold (Mo., day, yr.)	(d) Sales price (see page D-5)	(e) Cost or other basis (see page D-5)	(f) GAIN or (LOSS) Subtract (e) from (d)
1 NON-BUSINESS					
BAD DEBT	1998	1998	0	4,000	(4,000)

2 Enter your short-term totals, if any, from Schedule D-1, line 2	**2**			(4,000)
3 Total short-term sales price amounts. Add column (d) of lines 1 and 2 . .	**3**			
4 Short-term gain from Form 6252 and short-term gain or (loss) from Forms 4684, 6781, and 8824	**4**			
5 Net short-term gain or (loss) from partnerships, S corporations, estates, and trusts from Schedule(s) K-1	**5**			
6 Short-term capital loss carryover. Enter the amount, if any, from line 8 of your 1998 Capital Loss Carryover Worksheet	**6** (	)		
7 Net short-term capital gain or (loss). Combine lines 1 through 6 in column (f) ▶	**7**			(4,000)

Part II   Long-Term Capital Gains and Losses—Assets Held More Than One Year

(a) Description of property (Example: 100 sh. XYZ Co.)	(b) Date acquired (Mo., day, yr.)	(c) Date sold (Mo., day, yr.)	(d) Sales price (see page D-5)	(e) Cost or other basis (see page D-5)	(f) GAIN or (LOSS) Subtract (e) from (d)	(g) 28% RATE GAIN or (LOSS) (see instr. below)
8						

9 Enter your long-term totals, if any, from Schedule D-1, line 9	**9**				
10 Total long-term sales price amounts. Add column (d) of lines 8 and 9 . .	**10**				
11 Gain from Form 4797, Part I; long-term gain from Forms 2439 and 6252; and long-term gain or (loss) from Forms 4684, 6781, and 8824	**11**				
12 Net long-term gain or (loss) from partnerships, S corporations, estates, and trusts from Schedule(s) K-1.	**12**				
13 Capital gain distributions. See page D-1	**13**				
14 Long-term capital loss carryover. Enter in both columns (f) and (g) the amount, if any, from line 13 of your 1998 Capital Loss Carryover Worksheet	**14** (	) (	)		
15 Combine lines 8 through 14 in column (g)	**15**				
16 Net long-term capital gain or (loss). Combine lines 8 through 14 in column (f) ▶ Next: Go to Part III on the back.	**16**				

*28% Rate Gain or Loss includes all "collectibles gains and losses" (as defined on page D-5) and up to 50% of the eligible gain on qualified small business stock (see page D-4).

For Paperwork Reduction Act Notice, see Form 1040 instructions.   Cat. No. 11338H   Schedule D (Form 1040) 1999

Schedule D (Form 1040) 1999   Page **2**

Part III   Summary of Parts I and II

17 Combine lines 7 and 16. If a loss, go to line 18. If a gain, enter the gain on Form 1040, line 13   **17**   (4,000)

    Next: Complete Form 1040 through line 39. Then, go to **Part IV** to figure your tax if:
- Both lines 16 and 17 are gains, **and**
- Form 1040, line 39, is more than zero.

18 If line 17 is a loss, enter here and as a (loss) on Form 1040, line 13, the **smaller** of these losses:
- The loss on line 17, **or**
- ($3,000) or, if married filing separately, ($1,500) . . . .   **18** (3,000   )

    Next: Skip **Part IV** below. Instead, complete Form 1040 through line 37. Then, complete the **Capital Loss Carryover Worksheet** on page D-6 if:
- The loss on line 17 exceeds the loss on line 18, **or**
- Form 1040, line 37, is a loss.

Part IV   Tax Computation Using Maximum Capital Gains Rates

19 Enter your taxable income from Form 1040, line 39 . . . .   **19**

20 Enter the **smaller** of line 16 or line 17 of Schedule D **20**

21 If you are filing Form 4952, enter the amount from Form 4952, line 4e **21**

22 Subtract line 21 from line 20. If zero or less, enter -0- **22**

23 Combine lines 7 and 15. If zero or less, enter -0- **23**

24 Enter the **smaller** of line 15 or line 23, but not less than zero . . . **24**

25 Enter your unrecaptured section 1250 gain, if any, from line 16 of the worksheet on page D-7 . . . . **25**

26 Add lines 24 and 25 . . . . **26**

27 Subtract line 26 from line 22. If zero or less, enter -0- **27**

28 Subtract line 27 from line 19. If zero or less, enter -0- **28**

29 Enter the **smaller** of:
- The amount on line 19, **or**
- $25,750 if single; $43,050 if married filing jointly or qualifying widow(er); $21,525 if married filing separately; or $34,550 if head of household } **29**

30 Enter the **smaller** of line 28 or line 29 . . . . **30**

31 Subtract line 22 from line 19. If zero or less, enter -0- **31**

32 Enter the **larger** of line 30 or line 31 . . . . ▶ **32**

33 Figure the tax on the amount on line 32. Use the Tax Table or Tax Rate Schedules, whichever applies   **33**

    Note. If line 29 is less than line 28, go to line 38.

34 Enter the amount from line 29 . . . . **34**

35 Enter the amount from line 28 . . . . **35**

36 Subtract line 35 from line 34. If zero or less, enter -0- . . . . ▶ **36**

37 Multiply line 36 by 10% (.10) **37**

    Note. If line 27 is more than zero **and** equal to line 36, go to line 52.

38 Enter the **smaller** of line 19 or line 27 . . . . **38**

39 Enter the amount from line 36 . . . . **39**

40 Subtract line 39 from line 38 . . . . ▶ **40**

41 Multiply line 40 by 20% (.20) **41**

    Note. If line 25 is zero or blank, skip lines 42 through 47 and read the note above line 48.

42 Enter the **smaller** of line 22 or line 25 . . . . . . **42**

43 Add lines 22 and 32 . . . . . . **43**

44 Enter the amount from line 19 . . . **44**

45 Subtract line 44 from line 43. If zero or less, enter -0- **45**

46 Subtract line 45 from line 42. If zero or less, enter -0- . . . ▶ **46**

47 Multiply line 46 by 25% (.25) **47**

    Note. If line 24 is zero or blank, go to line 52.

48 Enter the amount from line 19 . . . **48**

49 Add lines 32, 36, 40, and 46 . . . **49**

50 Subtract line 49 from line 48 . . . **50**

51 Multiply line 50 by 28% (.28) **51**

52 Add lines 33, 37, 41, 47, and 51 . . . .   **52**

53 Figure the tax on the amount on line 19. Use the Tax Table or Tax Rate Schedules, whichever applies   **53**

54 **Tax on all taxable income (including capital gains).** Enter the **smaller** of line 52 or line 53 here and on Form 1040, line 40. . . . .   **54**

Chapter 7—Stock Options

We thought we would share one our favorite stories with you to illustrate how to report stock options. Phyllis went to work for a startup computer software company about 5 years ago. She was given 100 qualified stock options, each allowing her to buy the company's stock at $10 per share, which was what they were worth at that time. In early 1997, when they went up in value to $11, she exercised her options, buying the stock. In late 1999 (after she had held the stock for over a year, so it would be taxed at a lower tax rate), She sold the stock at $15 per share.

What were the tax consequences? When she got the options, there were no tax effects (this is true regardless of whether the options are qualified or non-qualified). When she exercised them in 1997, again no tax consequence (if these had been non-qualified, she would've reported it as wage income of $1 per share times 100 shares). When she sold the stock in 1999, she then reported it as a long-term capital gain, which in her setting, was taxed at only 10%!

A filled-out Schedule D, following, shows how she reports the option gains.

Form **1040**	Department of the Treasury—Internal Revenue Service		
	U.S. Individual Income Tax Return 19**99**	IRS Use Only—Do not write or staple in this space.	

For the year Jan. 1–Dec. 31, 1999, or other tax year beginning _____, 1999, ending _____   OMB No. 1545-0074

Label (See instructions on page 18.)

Your first name and initial: PHYLLIS   Last name   Your social security number

If a joint return, spouse's first name and initial   Last name   Spouse's social security number

Use the IRS label. Otherwise, please print or type.

Home address (number and street). If you have a P.O. box, see page 18.   Apt. no.

City, town or post office, state, and ZIP code. If you have a foreign address, see page 18.

▲ IMPORTANT! ▲ You must enter your SSN(s) above.

Presidential Election Campaign (See page 18.)
Do you want $3 to go to this fund?
If a joint return, does your spouse want $3 to go to this fund?

Yes | No | Note: Checking "Yes" will not change your tax or reduce your refund.

Filing Status — Check only one box.
1 Single
2 Married filing joint return (even if only one had income)
3 Married filing separate return. Enter spouse's social security no. above and full name here. ►
4 Head of household (with qualifying person). (See page 18.) If the qualifying person is a child but not your dependent, enter this child's name here. ►
5 Qualifying widow(er) with dependent child (year spouse died ► 19___). (See page 18.)

Exemptions
6a ☐ Yourself. If your parent (or someone else) can claim you as a dependent on his or her tax return, do not check box 6a
b ☐ Spouse
c Dependents:
(1) First name / Last name	(2) Dependent's social security number	(3) Dependent's relationship to you	(4) ✓ if qualifying child for child tax credit (see page 19)

d Total number of exemptions claimed

If more than six dependents, see page 19.

No. of boxes checked on 6a and 6b. No. of your children on 6c who: • lived with you • did not live with you due to divorce or separation (see page 18). Dependents on 6c not entered above. Add numbers entered on lines above ►

Income
Attach Copy B of your Forms W-2 and W-2G here. Also attach Form(s) 1099-R if tax was withheld.
If you did not get a W-2, see page 20.
Enclose, but do not staple, any payment. Also, please use Form 1040-V.

7	Wages, salaries, tips, etc. Attach Form(s) W-2	7	
8a	Taxable interest. Attach Schedule B if required	8a	
b	Tax-exempt interest. DO NOT include on line 8a . 8b		
9	Ordinary dividends. Attach Schedule B if required	9	
10	Taxable refunds, credits, or offsets of state and local income taxes (see page 21)	10	
11	Alimony received	11	
12	Business income or (loss). Attach Schedule C or C-EZ	12	
13	Capital gain or (loss). Attach Schedule D if required. If not required, check here ► ☐	13	500
14	Other gains or (losses). Attach Form 4797	14	
15a	Total IRA distributions 15a b Taxable amount (see page 22)	15b	
16a	Total pensions and annuities 16a b Taxable amount (see page 22)	16b	
17	Rental real estate, royalties, partnerships, S corporations, trusts, etc. Attach Schedule E	17	
18	Farm income or (loss). Attach Schedule F	18	
19	Unemployment compensation	19	
20a	Social security benefits 20a b Taxable amount (see page 24)	20b	
21	Other income. List type and amount (see page 24)	21	
22	Add the amounts in the far right column for lines 7 through 21. This is your **total income** ►	22	

Adjusted Gross Income
23	IRA deduction (see page 26)	23	
24	Student loan interest deduction (see page 26)	24	
25	Medical savings account deduction. Attach Form 8853	25	
26	Moving expenses. Attach Form 3903	26	
27	One-half of self-employment tax. Attach Schedule SE	27	
28	Self-employed health insurance deduction (see page 28)	28	
29	Keogh and self-employed SEP and SIMPLE plans	29	
30	Penalty on early withdrawal of savings	30	
31a	Alimony paid b Recipient's SSN ►	31a	
32	Add lines 23 through 31a	32	
33	Subtract line 32 from line 22. This is your **adjusted gross income** ►	33	

For Disclosure, Privacy Act, and Paperwork Reduction Act Notice, see page 54.   Cat. No. 11320B   Form **1040** (1999)

| SCHEDULE D (Form 1040) Department of the Treasury Internal Revenue Service (99) | Capital Gains and Losses
▶ Attach to Form 1040.   ▶ See Instructions for Schedule D (Form 1040).
▶ Use Schedule D-1 for more space to list transactions for lines 1 and 8. | | OMB No. 1545-0074
19**99**
Attachment
Sequence No. 12 |

Name(s) shown on Form 1040
PHYLLIS   Your social security number

Part I   Short-Term Capital Gains and Losses—Assets Held One Year or Less

(a) Description of property (Example: 100 sh. XYZ Co.)	(b) Date acquired (Mo., day, yr.)	(c) Date sold (Mo., day, yr.)	(d) Sales price (see page D-5)	(e) Cost or other basis (see page D-5)	(f) GAIN or (LOSS) Subtract (e) from (d)	
1						

2 Enter your short-term totals, if any, from Schedule D-1, line 2		**2**				
3 **Total short-term sales price amounts.** Add column (d) of lines 1 and 2		**3**				
4 Short-term gain from Form 6252 and short-term gain or (loss) from Forms 4684, 6781, and 8824				**4**		
5 Net short-term gain or (loss) from partnerships, S corporations, estates, and trusts from Schedule(s) K-1				**5**		
6 Short-term capital loss carryover. Enter the amount, if any, from line 8 of your 1998 Capital Loss Carryover Worksheet				**6**	(	)
7 **Net short-term capital gain or (loss).** Combine lines 1 through 6 in column (f) ▶				**7**		

Part II   Long-Term Capital Gains and Losses—Assets Held More Than One Year

(a) Description of property (Example: 100 sh. XYZ Co.)	(b) Date acquired (Mo., day, yr.)	(c) Date sold (Mo., day, yr.)	(d) Sales price (see page D-5)	(e) Cost or other basis (see page D-5)	(f) GAIN or (LOSS) Subtract (e) from (d)	(g) 28% RATE GAIN or (LOSS) (see instr. below)
8						
100 SHARES						
COMPANY STOCK	1997	1999	1500	1000	500	

9 Enter your long-term totals, if any, from Schedule D-1, line 9		**9**				
10 **Total long-term sales price amounts.** Add column (d) of lines 8 and 9		**10**				
11 Gain from Form 4797, Part I; long-term gain from Forms 2439 and 6252; and long-term gain or (loss) from Forms 4684, 6781, and 8824				**11**		
12 Net long-term gain or (loss) from partnerships, S corporations, estates, and trusts from Schedule(s) K-1.				**12**		
13 Capital gain distributions. See page D-1				**13**		
14 Long-term capital loss carryover. Enter in both columns (f) and (g) the amount, if any, from line 13 of your 1998 Capital Loss Carryover Worksheet				**14** (	) (	)
15 Combine lines 8 through 14 in column (g).				**15**		
16 **Net long-term capital gain or (loss).** Combine lines 8 through 14 in column (f) ▶ Next: Go to Part III on the back.				**16**		

* **28% Rate Gain or Loss** includes **all** "collectibles gains and losses" (as defined on page D-5) and up to 50% of the eligible gain on qualified small business stock (see page D-4).

For Paperwork Reduction Act Notice, see Form 1040 instructions.   Cat. No. 11338H   Schedule D (Form 1040) 1999

Schedule D (Form 1040) 1998   Page **2**

Part III	**Summary of Parts I and II**		

17 Combine lines 7 and 16. If a loss, go to line 18. If a gain, enter the gain on Form 1040, line 13 | **17** | |

Next: Complete Form 1040 through line 39. Then, go to **Part IV** to figure your tax if:
  • Both lines 16 and 17 are gains, **and**
  • Form 1040, line 39, is more than zero.

18 If line 17 is a loss, enter here and as a (loss) on Form 1040, line 13, the **smaller** of these losses:
  • The loss on line 17; **or**
  • ($3,000) or, if married filing separately, ($1,500) . . . . | **18** |(|)

Next: Complete Form 1040 through line 37. Then, complete the **Capital Loss Carryover Worksheet** on page D-6 if:
  • The loss on line 17 exceeds the loss on line 18, **or**
  • Form 1040, line 37, is a loss.

Part IV	**Tax Computation Using Maximum Capital Gains Rates**		

19 Enter your taxable income from Form 1040, line 39 . . . . | **19** | |

20 Enter the **smaller** of line 16 or line 17 of Schedule D . . . . . | **20** |

21 If you are filing Form 4952, enter the amount from Form 4952, line 4e | **21** |

22 Subtract line 21 from line 20. If zero or less, enter -0- . . . . . . | **22** |

23 Combine lines 7 and 15. If zero or less, enter -0- . . . . | **23** |

24 Enter the **smaller** of line 15 or line 23, but not less than zero . . . | **24** |

25 Enter your unrecaptured section 1250 gain, if any (see page D-7) . | **25** |

26 Add lines 24 and 25 . . . . | **26** |

27 Subtract line 26 from line 22. If zero or less, enter -0- . . . . | **27** |

28 Subtract line 27 from line 19. If zero or less, enter -0- . . . . | **28** |

29 Enter the **smaller** of:
  • The amount on line 19, **or**
  • $25,350 if single; $42,350 if married filing jointly or qualifying widow(er); $21,175 if married filing separately; or $33,950 if head of household . . . . . | **29** |

30 Enter the **smaller** of line 28 or line 29 . . . . | **30** |

31 Subtract line 22 from line 19. If zero or less, enter -0- . . . . | **31** |

32 Enter the **larger** of line 30 or line 31 . . . . | **32** |

33 Figure the tax on the amount on line 32. Use the Tax Table or Tax Rate Schedules, whichever applies . . . . ▶ | **33** |

34 Enter the amount from line 29 . . . . | **34** |

35 Enter the amount from line 28 . . . . | **35** |

36 Subtract line 35 from line 34. If zero or less, enter -0- . . . . | **36** |

37 Multiply line 36 by 10% (.10) . . . . ▶ | **37** | 50

38 Enter the **smaller** of line 19 or line 27 . . . . | **38** | 50

39 Enter the amount from line 36 . . . . | **39** |

40 Subtract line 39 from line 38 . . . . | **40** |

41 Multiply line 40 by 20% (.20) . . . . ▶ | **41** |

42 Enter the **smaller** of line 22 or line 25 . . . . | **42** |

43 Add lines 22 and 32 . . . . | **43** |

44 Enter the amount from line 19 . . . . | **44** |

45 Subtract line 44 from line 43. If zero or less, enter -0- . . . . | **45** |

46 Subtract line 45 from line 42. If zero or less, enter -0- . . . . | **46** |

47 Multiply line 46 by 25% (.25) . . . . ▶ | **47** |

48 Enter the amount from line 19 . . . . | **48** |

49 Add lines 32, 36, 40, and 46 . . . . | **49** |

50 Subtract line 49 from line 48 . . . . | **50** |

51 Multiply line 50 by 28% (.28) . . . . ▶ | **51** |

52 Add lines 33, 37, 41, 47, and 51 . . . . | **52** |

53 Figure the tax on the amount on line 19. Use the Tax Table or Tax Rate Schedules, whichever applies | **53** |

54 **Tax on taxable income (including capital gains).** Enter the **smaller** of line 52 or line 53 here and on Form 1040, line 40 . . . . ▶ | **54** | 50

Chapter 8—Retirement

Let's take a look at how Kim deducts the money she puts in her pension plan. Remember that her cosmetics business was a sole proprietorship, which she later converted to a corporation. Now, we're not going to show you how to report anything on a corporate income tax return; you really need a tax practitioner to fill out the form 1120.

What we can show you is how she deducted her contributions to her defined contribution plan the year just before she changed into a corporation.[18] Like all unincorporated businesses, things are reported on a Schedule C, which attaches to your long-form 1040. Kim's Schedule C is on the following page.

---

18 Now, you don't have to incorporate to get the tax benefits of this type of plan. We had Kim incorporate for other business reasons.

SCHEDULE C
(Form 1040)

Department of the Treasury
Internal Revenue Service   (99)

Profit or Loss From Business
(Sole Proprietorship)

▶ Partnerships, joint ventures, etc., must file Form 1065 or Form 1065-B.

▶ Attach to Form 1040 or Form 1041.   ▶ See Instructions for Schedule C (Form 1040).

OMB No. 1545-0074

1999

Attachment
Sequence No. **09**

Name of proprietor

KIM

Social security number (SSN)

A	Principal business or profession, including product or service (see page C-1)		B Enter code from pages C-8 & 9 ▶
C	Business name. If no separate business name, leave blank		D Employer ID number (EIN), if any

E Business address (including suite or room no.) ▶
  City, town or post office, state, and ZIP code

F Accounting method: (1) ☐ Cash   (2) ☐ Accrual   (3) ☐ Other (specify) ▶

G Did you "materially participate" in the operation of this business during 1999? If "No," see page C-2 for limit on losses   ☐ Yes ☐ No

H If you started or acquired this business during 1999, check here   ▶ ☐

Part I   Income

1	Gross receipts or sales. **Caution:** *If this income was reported to you on Form W-2 and the "Statutory employee" box on that form was checked, see page C-2 and check here* ▶ ☐	1	
2	Returns and allowances	2	
3	Subtract line 2 from line 1	3	
4	Cost of goods sold (from line 42 on page 2)	4	
5	**Gross profit.** Subtract line 4 from line 3	5	
6	Other income, including Federal and state gasoline or fuel tax credit or refund (see page C-3)	6	
7	**Gross income.** Add lines 5 and 6 ▶	7	

Part II   Expenses. Enter expenses for business use of your home **only** on line 30.

8	Advertising	8		19 Pension and profit-sharing plans	19	30,000
9	Bad debts from sales or services (see page C-3)	9		20 Rent or lease (see page C-4):		
				a Vehicles, machinery, and equipment	20a	
10	Car and truck expenses (see page C-3)	10		b Other business property	20b	
11	Commissions and fees	11		21 Repairs and maintenance	21	
12	Depletion	12		22 Supplies (not included in Part III)	22	
13	Depreciation and section 179 expense deduction (not included in Part III) (see page C-3)	13		23 Taxes and licenses	23	
				24 Travel, meals, and entertainment:		
14	Employee benefit programs (other than on line 19)	14		a Travel	24a	
15	Insurance (other than health)	15		b Meals and entertainment		
16	Interest:			c Enter nondeductible amount included on line 24b (see page C-5)		
a	Mortgage (paid to banks, etc.)	16a		d Subtract line 24c from line 24b	24d	
b	Other	16b		25 Utilities	25	
17	Legal and professional services	17		26 Wages (less employment credits)	26	
18	Office expense	18		27 Other expenses (from line 48 on page 2)	27	

28	**Total expenses** before expenses for business use of home. Add lines 8 through 27 in columns ▶	28	
29	Tentative profit (loss). Subtract line 28 from line 7	29	
30	Expenses for business use of your home. Attach Form 8829	30	
31	**Net profit or (loss).** Subtract line 30 from line 29.		
	• If a profit, enter on **Form 1040, line 12**, and ALSO on **Schedule SE, line 2** (statutory employees, see page C-6). Estates and trusts, enter on Form 1041, line 3.	31	
	• If a loss, you MUST go on to line 32.		
32	If you have a loss, check the box that describes your investment in this activity (see page C-6).		
	• If you checked 32a, enter the loss on **Form 1040, line 12**, and ALSO on **Schedule SE, line 2** (statutory employees, see page C-6). Estates and trusts, enter on Form 1041, line 3.	32a ☐ All investment is at risk. 32b ☐ Some investment is not	
	• If you checked 32b, you MUST attach Form 6198.	at risk.	

For Paperwork Reduction Act Notice, see Form 1040 instructions.   Cat. No. 11334P   Schedule C (Form 1040) 1999